The
Liturgical
Ministry
Series®

GUIDE FOR CANTORS

SECOND EDITION

Jennifer Kerr Breedlove
Paul Turner

LTP
LITURGY
TRAINING
PUBLICATIONS

Nihil Obstat
Very Reverend Daniel A. Smilanic, JCD
Vicar for Canonical Services
Archdiocese of Chicago
December 18, 2013

Imprimatur
Most Reverend Francis J. Kane, DD
Vicar General
Archdiocese of Chicago
December 18, 2013

THE LITURGICAL MINISTRY SERIES®: GUIDE FOR CANTORS, SECOND EDITION © 2014 Archdiocese of Chicago: Liturgy Training Publications, 3949 South Racine Avenue, Chicago IL 60609; 1-800-933-1800, fax 1-800-933-7094, e-mail orders@ltp.org. All rights reserved. See our Web site at www.LTP.org.

Cover photo by Anna Manhart. Interior photos by John Zich. Music engraved by James T. Gerber.

Printed in the United States of America.

Library of Congress Control Number: 2013957613

17 16 15 14   1 2 3 4

ISBN 978-1-61671-182-5

ELCAN2

Psalm 98:1b–6

O sing a new song to the LORD,
for he has worked wonders.
His right hand and his holy arm
have brought salvation.

The LORD has made known his salvation,
has shown his deliverance to the nations.
He has remembered his merciful love
and his truth for the house of Irsael.

All the ends of the earth have seen
the salvation of our God.
Shout to the LORD, all the earth;
break forth into joyous song,
and sing out your praise.

Sing psalms the Lord with the harp,
with the harp and the sound of song.
With trumpets and the sound of the horn,
raise a shout before the King, the LORD.

Table of Contents

Preface

Then, after singing a hymn, they went out to the Mount of Olives.

—*Matthew 26:30*

One of Jesus's disciples was a cantor. Maybe even more than one. We don't know who it was. The Gospels never tell us. But whenever the disciples prayed together, somebody had to lead the singing. On most days, the duty would have been a great joy. Who wouldn't want to lead a hymn and sing along with Jesus?

But the disciples also had to sing on days they didn't feel like singing. On some days Jesus preached when no one listened. On other days the disciples grew tired from managing the crowds seeking cures. On still other days Jesus disputed with religious leaders. Or he corrected his followers. Or he cursed a fig tree.

The disciples didn't always feel like singing.

They probably had a repertoire of music commonly known by other Jewish worshippers of their time and place. The Book of Psalms was their main hymnal. They knew the music as well as people today know the national anthem, the birthday song, and Christmas carols. Everyone could join in. But they needed someone to start the singing. They needed a cantor.

The Gospels make one explicit reference to the singing of the disciples. It took place at the Last Supper.

One year, on the first day of the Feast of Unleavened Bread, some of the disciples asked Jesus, "Where do you want us to prepare for you to eat the Passover?"[1] They might have asked him that question every year. They may not have realized that this was to be the last year—the last week, the last day, and the final hour.

Jesus sent them into Jerusalem to a particular man in a particular house to deliver this message: "My appointed time draws near; in your house I shall celebrate the Passover with my disciples."[2]

Did the disciples understand what this meal would be? Or were they just trying to get dinner organized?

The Passover is a beautiful meal of faith and prayer. But this one started off on a very ominous note. Jesus looked at his dinner companions and distressed them all with this announcement: "One of you will betray me."[3]

This was not going to be an ordinary meal. One by one the disciples asked him, "Surely it is not I, Lord?"[4] They all wondered. Peter wondered. The sons of Zebedee wondered. The beloved disciple wondered. The cantor wondered. "Surely it is not I, Rabbi?"[5] Judas asked. Jesus said, "You have said so."[6]

The meal became more mysterious. Jesus passed broken bread to his disciples and said, " 'Take and eat; this is my body.' Then he took a cup, gave thanks, and gave it to them saying, 'Drink from it, all of you, for this is my blood of the covenant.'"[7]

Did the disciples understand this? Did they realize this was the night before the day Jesus would die?

Filled with questions, distress, and awe, the cantor ate and drank the Body and Blood of the Lord for the first time. The disciples couldn't have known what to say. They had questions they dared not ask. Perhaps they did not feel like singing. Or perhaps they felt they had to sing. No one had ever been in this situation before. So the cantor did what cantors do. The cantor sang. And all joined in. "Then, after singing a hymn, they went out to the Mount of Olives."[8]

Paul Turner

NOTES

1. Matthew 26:17.

2. Ibid., 26:18.

3. Ibid., 26:21.

4. Ibid., 26:22.

5. Ibid., 26:25.

6. Ibid.

7. Ibid., 26:26–27.

8. Ibid., 26:30.

Welcome

You are serving your faith community as a cantor. God has given you a voice, and you are offering it back as an instrument of praise. You will express your own faith. You will help other believers pray in times of distress and times of joy. You will give voice to the songs of the Church.

Your ministry is an essential part of the Church's worship. It will serve the flow of liturgical prayer. It will add beauty and artistry to the way people pray. It will enliven the words that express belief and immerse those who sing them into the mystery of God.

Your role is known by different titles.

- You may be called a **song leader**. A song leader helps or animates all members of the assembly sing their parts together by setting the pitch and tempo, and inviting their singing with gestures or expressions of encouragement.

- You may be called a **psalmist**. A psalmist sings the verses of the Responsorial Psalm, adopting a role like that of the lector who reads the Word of God. You may even lead the psalm from the ambo, where the other Scriptures are proclaimed.

- Or you may be called the **cantor**, the one who leads others, sings solo verses, or alternates with a choir, and who holds together the sung music of common worship.

In all cases, you are the one with a skill to sing, a desire to lead, a love for the people, and a faith-filled heart that must praise God.

About the Book

This book will help you reflect on your ministry. It will not teach you new songs. It will not help you read music. These musical skills are important, but this book is about your ministry.

In these pages you will learn about the importance of liturgical music, how it serves the prayer of God's people, and how the ministry of cantor developed. It will answer your questions about many practical matters in the execution of your ministry. Above all it will help form you as a person of faith who will lead others in the purpose of liturgical song: giving praise to God.

About the Authors

This book was written by two authors. Paul Turner wrote the first sections of the book: the preface, "Welcome," "Theology and History of the Ministry," and "Spirituality and Formation of the Cantor." He is the pastor of St. Anthony Parish in Kansas City, Missouri. A priest of the diocese of Kansas City–St. Joseph, he holds a doctorate in sacred theology from Sant'Anselmo in Rome. He is the author of many pastoral resources about sacraments and the liturgy.

Jennifer Kerr Breedlove wrote the practical description and explanation of the cantor's duties in "Serving as a Cantor" and has provided the resources section and the glossary. She is best known in the Chicago area as a liturgical musician, conductor, and cantor, and is a widely published and recorded composer and arranger of liturgical music. She holds a masters' degree in theology from Catholic Theological Union and one in Choral Conducting from Indiana University, where she also taught music theory and sight-singing classes. She is currently completing her doctorate in Choral Conducting from Northwestern University.

During her years as director for Liturgical Music at the Office for Divine Worship, Jennifer served as conductor and cantor at many Chicago-area liturgical events. As conductor of the Jubilee Archdiocesan Choir and Jubilee 2000 Symphony Orchestra, she helped to plan and lead the music at the "Field of Faith" Jubilee celebration at Soldier Field in June of 2000. Jennifer is involved in a number of Chicago area ensembles, including the Chicago Symphony Chorus and the Cathedral Singers, and currently serves as an adjunct professor of Choral Music at St. Xavier University on the part-time choral faculty at North Central College in Naperville.

Questions for Discussion and Reflection

1. Why have you agreed to serve as a cantor?

_____

_____

_____

_____

_____

2. What do you hope to gain in your understanding of the theology and function of the ministry through this book?

_____

_____

_____

_____

_____

Theology and History of the Cantor

Singing is for one who loves.

—*St. Augustine*

Music in the Church and in Our Lives

"Singing is for one who loves." That bit of wisdom, taken from one of the sermons of St. Augustine, is quoted in the *General Instruction of the Roman Missal* (GIRM) as one reason we have liturgical music.[1] Listen to music on almost any radio station and you'll hear about love. Love is the one theme that unites the lyrics of almost all the songs. That theme recurs because listeners like to hear about love, but also because composers and singers have experienced it. Their hearts have been moved by eternal love, surprised by charitable love, hurt by rejected love, stunted by unreturned love, and frozen by unexpressed love. The emotions run so high that writers and singers have to do something about it. Words alone cannot express the feelings inside. They need music.

Many couples claim a song that becomes *their* song. If you have experienced the emotions expressed in a song that you hear, you may sing along with the radio or hum the tune in the car. "Singing is for one who loves."

Christians are in love with God. God is the center of our lives. The First Letter of John proclaims that "God is love."[2] The more deeply we appreciate the holiness of God, the nearness of God, and the love of God, the more we need to express how we feel. Words alone cannot do it. We need music.

Human beings are made for music. Our hearts beat in rhythm. Our voices modulate to speak our thoughts. At church we do the ordinary things we are made for. We greet one another. We speak. We listen. We eat. We drink. And we sing.

But these ordinary human activities take on an extraordinary dimension. We greet one another as the body of Christ. We speak words of acclamation and blessing. We listen to the holy Word of God. We eat the Bread of Life. We drink the cup of salvation. And we sing music that lifts our thoughts to heaven's throne.

Bound to the earth, we still participate in divine life. We already experience God among us, even as we wait to experience God perfectly at the end of time. The New Testament expresses how we live in hope, yet we experience Christ now. Most beautifully, the Letter to the Colossians says, "Let the word of Christ dwell in you richly, as in all wisdom you teach and admonish one another, singing psalms, hymns, and spiritual songs with gratitude in your hearts to God. And whatever you do, in word or in deed, do everything in the name of the Lord Jesus, giving thanks to God the Father through him."[3]

Christ dwells within us richly, and we sing our thanks.

Singing is essential to our worship. "Great importance should therefore be attached to the use of singing in the celebration of the Mass, with due consideration for the culture of peoples and abilities of each liturgical assembly."[4] With careful preparation and focused execution, the music during Mass will beautifully express the sentiments of those who worship.

Although the Mass is an ancient form of prayer, it continues to be offered through the lips and hearts of generations who live through changes in climes and cultures. The music we sing captures the past as well as the present. Those who sing proclaim a faith revealed in ages past, but they do so in songs expressing their faith in the midst of a changing world.

> ✛ Great importance should therefore be attached to the use of singing in the celebration of the Mass, with due consideration for the culture of peoples and abilities of each liturgical assembly.
>
> —*General Instruction of the Roman Missal*, 40

The Mass therefore permits various styles of music. "The main place should be given, all things being equal, to Gregorian chant"[5] because of its long historical association with the Roman liturgy. But other forms of music may be used, "provided that they correspond to the spirit of the liturgical action and that they foster the participation of all the faithful."[6] Musical styles develop, and many of them prove most useful for communal worship.

Some music is sung by all together. Other music is sung by a cantor or a choir. Sometimes the cantor sings verses while everyone else repeats a refrain. Sometimes the cantor alternates with the people so that every-one sings a while and listens a while to the Word of God in song.

Some music accompanies ritual actions. Other music has its own special place within the rite. For example, several processions happen to the accompa-niment of music: A procession of ministers enters the sanctuary while everyone sings. Before the Gospel is proclaimed, ministers process to the ambo while an acclamation is sung. The bread, wine, and gifts for the Church and the poor are often brought to the altar while music is played or sung. All those participating in Holy Communion process to the altar while the community sings its joy for the sacrament of the Lord's Body and Blood.

Some music accompanies ritual actions. Here we see the opening procession accompanied by the Entrance chant.

At other times, however, nothing happens besides the music. All other action stops during the Gloria, the Responsorial Psalm, and the dialogues and acclamations during the Eucharistic Prayer. Such music has its own place in the parts of the Mass. It does not accompany some other action; it demands the full attention of worshippers.

Music, then, connects to the liturgy in various ways. It is the pulse that drives the rhythm of the Mass. It is the thread that joins the parts. It creates moods that evoke prayer, praise, sorrow, and wonderment. It draws us closer to the mystery of the beauty of God.

The Role of the Cantor

The cantor works with the music to achieve its aims. The cantor is a leader. The cantor is to "direct and support the people's singing" and "to lead the different chants."[7]

> ✚ It is fitting that there be a cantor or a choir director to direct and support the people's singing.
>
> —*General Instruction of the Roman Missal*, 104

When sustaining "the people's singing," the cantor's voice should not overly predominate. The singing of the assembly is the voice that should be heard. The cantor may be needed to set the tone and pace, to summon the people into worship, to indicate that another verse is to begin, to keep the pitch where it belongs, and to monitor the rhythm of the music. But once an assembly develops these skills, the cantor's voice can back away. Especially when people sing music they know well, the cantor serves the community's voice by letting it be heard.

Cantors need to develop good musical skills, but during the Mass these skills are at the service of the liturgy. Cantors should learn how to read notes and how to interpret a piece of music. They hear liturgical music whenever they can, by attending parish and diocesan events or listening to recordings. They learn how to care for their instrument—the human voice. They protect it from illness. They warm up with exer-

cises. They practice proper breathing techniques. They learn how to sing loudly and softly, and how to recognize which volume is appropriate.

Cantors will develop their musical training. They will work with a teacher or with other cantors. They listen to professional singers. They learn about various styles of music and the skills required for each of them. They discern what kind of music fits their own voice, and they develop an interest in it.

As with any skill, music takes

At times during the Mass, nothing happens besides the music. Here we see a cantor leading the Gloria.

practice. Those who work on it every day develop an ear and a voice for their art. Every musician makes mistakes, but good musicians practice to keep them at a minimum.

Cantors sing in front of people, so they also need the ability to remain comfortable and composed. If the cantor has practiced well, he or she will relax into the role while others are listening, watching, or singing along. If the cantor is relaxed, everyone else will be too.

Still, after giving all this attention to the art of music, being a cantor is different from being a performer. Many performances draw the attention of people to the performers, but the cantor draws the attention of the people to God, the Creator of everything—of humans, of their voices, and of music.

This distinction helps many cantors relax. If they feel they lack some musical skill, they are comforted that they possess a strong and lively faith. If the goal of liturgical music is to share faith, many find that easier to attain than the goal of singing well.

Still, a cantor should not neglect the development of musical skill. God has given the talent, and he expects it to be developed and used. Among the parables of Jesus is one about "talents."[8] A master going on a journey entrusts his servants with talents according to their ability. The word "talent" in the parable refers to a kind of money. But the same word evolved into a word meaning "ability" because those with abilities often became "talented" and prospered economically. In the parable, the master returns and finds that only two of his servants doubled their money. He told them, "Come, share your master's joy."[9] But he was so disappointed with the third servant, who hid the talent, that the master took the talent away and threw the servant out.

God gives gifts for a purpose. We are to develop them and put them to use for the sake of the Church.

Even so, one of the skills a cantor develops is the skill of faith. Even if a cantor can sing all the notes correctly and pronounce all the words distinctly, the cantor still needs to sing with faith. Some of the most accomplished singers cannot do it, but some of the least can.

One skill of faith is the ability to manage silences. Just as any melody needs rests to define its character, so the Mass needs silence to define its spoken and sung sounds. A cantor will often be expected to hold the community in silent prayer—before singing the Kyrie, beginning the Responsorial Psalm, or introducing the Acclamation before the Gospel, for example. At other times the music begins immediately upon a cue: the *Sanctus* (Holy, Holy, Holy), the memorial acclamation, and the Amen, for example. The cantor will need to balance silence, acclamation, and pacing to let the music fit the overarching rhythm of the Mass.

The cantor is one of many ministers at the Eucharist. A priest presides at worship. A deacon assists. Lectors and readers proclaim the Scriptures. Extraordinary ministers of Holy Communion assist the orderly sharing of the Body and Blood of Christ. Ushers, greeters, and hospitality ministers help people feel at home. Servers keep the liturgy flowing smoothly. The assembly puts its heart and voice into the words and actions of the Mass.

This diversity of ministries shows the activity of the Holy Spirit, who bestows all gifts in abundance. Every worshipping community possesses many gifts. Some people may be unaware of their gifts. When they discover them and offer what they have, their participation enlivens their faith, and the whole community bears witness to the manifold presence of the Holy Spirit. When all these gifts work together for a common purpose, the marvels of the Holy Spirit are plain to see.

This miraculous presence of the Holy Spirit was evident from the earliest days of the Church. St. Paul wrote that "there are different kinds of spiritual gifts but the same Spirit; there are different forms of service but the same Lord; there are different workings but the same God who produces all of them in everyone. To each individual the manifestation of the Spirit is given for some benefit."[10]

Thus, this diversity of gifts shows the unity of the Body of Christ. The cantor's gifts are intended to foster that unity. God has given special gifts to the cantor, but they are given "for some benefit"[11]—for the manifestation of the Spirit of God to the entire assembly of believers.

Good cantors will contribute the gifts God gave them and encourage the gifts of others. Some people struggle to use their gifts in a meaningful way. Their talents may not be appreciated by others, but their faith and desire to serve always is. Good cantors will assist the work of the Holy Spirit by summoning forth the gifts of the community and helping individuals develop them.

In the end, the gathered faithful express their unity by offering their gifts, and they achieve deeper unity by appreciating the gifts of others. "There should be harmony and diligence among all those involved in the effective preparation of each liturgical celebration in accordance with the Missal and other liturgical books, both as regards the rites and as regards the pastoral and musical aspects."[12] "Harmony and diligence" are two skills that good musicians know well.[13] Cantors are naturally disposed to contribute to the harmony of the body of Christ.

> *There are different kinds of spiritual gifts but the same Spirit; there are different forms of service but the same Lord; there are different workings but the same God who produces all of them in everyone. To each individual the manifestation of the Spirit is given for some benefit.*
>
> —1 Corinthians 12:4–7

> ✚ There should be harmony and diligence among all those involved in the effective preparation of each liturgical celebraiton in accordance with the Missal, and other liturgical books, both as regards the rites and as regards the pastoral and musical aspects.
>
> —General Instruction of the Roman Missal, 111

After all, cantors are part of the assembly of the faithful. They come to Mass with the same intention as every other worshipper: to give praise and glory to God, to listen to the sacred writings, and to share in Holy Communion. As a member of the faithful, the cantor has prepared for this Mass with a life devoted to the teachings of Christ, and the cantor leaves the celebration with the commission to bring the word of Christ everywhere throughout the coming week.

Members of the assembly focus their attention on the texts and actions of the Mass in order to participate well and to take full advantage of the gift of Christ. Cantors also focus their attention on the whole of the Mass. They participate throughout, even in the parts that do not directly involve their voice. They call to mind their sins. They listen attentively to the readings. During the Eucharistic Prayer, they join their hearts and thoughts to the words spoken by the priest.

Participating during Mass demands a lot of attention. Members of the assembly fight distractions to their prayer every week. Cantors do, too. Cantors can be easily distracted by the practical demands of their ministry. Is the hymn board properly marked? Have they coordinated with the organist about the number of verses to be sung? Do they remember how the psalm tone for this week goes? Will they be able to find the page for the Gloria immediately after singing the entrance song? Cantors shuffle paper during Mass. If they draw too much attention to themselves, or if their attention drifts from the unfolding liturgy, they withdraw from the service. They become focused on themselves and the timely execution of their work, rather than on the flow of the Mass.

In a sense the cantor never has a break during the Eucharist because he or she is a member of the assembly. No one has a break during Mass. At times each member of the assembly has something to say or do, but at other times each member listens and reflects. There is always something to do, and cantors are called to participate in nonmusical moments as energetically as they do when they sing.

When cantors participate well, they become a model for the rest of the community. Cantors have a lot to manage during Mass, but if even they can participate in everything, they give hope and guidance to the other worshippers in the room. Cantors are people of faith.

The History of the Cantor

The book that most influenced the history of cantors was the Psalter. The Book of Psalms is popularly attributed to King David, but it was probably written anonymously by a number of people over a period of centuries. It was formed like a modern hymnal. It included some songs that had been sung for generations, some that had been more recently composed, and some that were known in different geographical areas.

No one knows what the music of the psalms first sounded like. Attempts have been made to reconstruct the sound, based on knowledge of instruments and language. But no one knows for sure.

The texts of the psalms suggest that some were led by one person, others by a group. Some of the psalms were too long for everyone to sing them by memory (for example, 106). A few have refrains, indicating that everyone sang those words while someone else sang verses (for example, 67). Some of the texts accompanied processions (for example, 122). Others meditate on the goodness of God's law (for example, 119). Some develop a theme (for example, 23, "The Lord is my shepherd"). Others function like an alphabetical acrostic: Each line begins with a successive letter of the Hebrew alphabet (for example, 34). The psalms probably needed a skilled singer, but they were popular enough to be remembered for generations.

The psalms provided the backbone for Jewish worship, which in turn inspired Christian prayer. Christians increasingly viewed the psalms as prophetic. Some lines foreshadow the coming of Christ, his ministry, Death, and Resurrection. Consequently, the psalms have become very dear to Christian worship.

By the fourth century, cantors and singers were so popular in some churches that regulations came into play. A council in Laodicea permitted cantors to sing at the ambo from specially prepared parchments, but they were not to wear the same vestments as other ministers. The same council also restricted ministers—including singers—from patronizing local taverns. From the earliest days skilled ministers were expected to lead moral lives, so that their behavior outside church would enhance their ministry in church.

As the liturgy became more complex, the sung texts multiplied. Music was needed for processions, dialogues, and acclamations. Skilled singers were needed to lead the singing.

Monasticism developed, and monasteries of nuns and monks devoted many hours each week to singing the psalms. The music needed leadership. Cantors intoned psalms and sang verses.

✠ The main place should be given, all things being equal, to Gregorian chant, as being proper to the Roman Liturgy.

—*General Instruction of the Roman Missal*, 41

These musical needs led to the development of Gregorian chant. Music was composed, a system of notation was devised, singers were trained, and a great body of music circulated throughout the Christian world. It took hundreds of years, and the style of chant changed very little during that time. The Gregorian chants for the Liturgy of the Hours and of the Eucharist formed one of the most influential bodies of compositions in the entire history of music. To be sung, the chants needed well-trained choirs, and they needed cantors.[14]

In time, musical styles developed from the unaccompanied melodies of chant to the intricate polyphonic music of the Renaissance. In many places the work of the cantor was taken over by choirs. In Masses without music the priest often recited the lines that would have been sung by others.

With the liturgical movement of the twentieth century, congregational singing returned to Catholic worship. Cantors began to assist by announcing hymns and leading the singing. With the invention of microphones and speakers, a cantor's voice could be heard throughout a church more loudly than ever before.

As the Book of Psalms influenced the development of liturgical music, the Responsorial Psalm restored the cantor to a place of prominence. The reforms of the Second Vatican Council expanded the music that used to follow the First Reading during Mass. Prior to that time, someone sang or read a couple lines of Scripture, known as the gradual or the tract, and coupled it with an Alleluia. But the Council expanded the number of Sunday readings from two to three, offered the Responsorial Psalm as an alternative to the gradual, and separated the Alleluia out to become a separate piece of music.

The Council also divided *The Roman Missal* into two volumes. For the first time in many centuries, the Lectionary appeared in a separate book. As Lectionaries went to press, a Responsorial Psalm was printed for each Mass. Actually, the psalm was just one option. It was still permitted to sing the gradual. But the Responsorial Psalm was so popular that it appeared alone in Lectionaries and became widely used throughout the Catholic world.

The psalm needed a cantor. The Responsorial Psalm could be, has been, and is being recited during many Masses. But it was designed to be sung. The psalms themselves were composed as lyrics, and their appearance in the Lectionary intended to expand the music after the First Reading.

The psalms in the Lectionary are all responsorial, that is, they all contain an antiphon to be sung by the people. In the Bible, however, very few of the psalms are responsorial by nature. Most of them develop a single idea from start to finish. The Lectionary changed the structure of virtually every psalm by turning them into responsories. It also abbreviated many psalms so the responsories maintain a similar length.

These changes made it possible for people to sing a new piece of music every week, while giving them a refrain that made the psalm their own. The refrain puts the ancient words on the lips of modern worshippers. It develops the prophetic nature of the psalms that Christians find so dear. By singing the refrain today, the assembly proclaims that this psalm is not just a piece of musical history. It does not merely address a situation that happened long ago. It addresses something happening now, here, in this church with these singers. The Holy Spirit, so active in the writer of this psalm long ago, is still active in the hearts of those who sing it today.

By assigning the verses of the psalm to a cantor, the liturgy permits a wide variety of musical forms to be used for this part of the Mass. The cantor sings the verses in a way that illumines the hearts of the people and draws them deeper into the mystery of God's Word.

Consequently, the role of the cantor has developed significantly over many centuries. It has been restored to a central place in Catholic worship. The cantor leads the singing of the assembly. The cantor sings the psalm. God has blessed the cantor with musical gifts. The cantor inspires others with a faith so strong that it must be voiced in song.

Questions for Discussion and Reflection

1. How do you prepare to participate during Mass?

_____

_____

_____

_____

_____

_____

2. What moves you most when you pray during Mass?

_____

_____

_____

_____

_____

3. What are the talents that God has given you? How are you returning them?

_____

_____

_____

_____

_____

_____

4. What pieces of music help you express your faith?

_____

_____

_____

_____

_____

NOTES

1. *General Instruction of the Roman Missal* (GIRM), 39.

2. 1 John 4:8.

3. Colossians 3:16–17.

4. GIRM, 40.

5. Ibid., 41.

6. Ibid.

7. GIRM, 104.

8. See Matthew 25:14–30.

9. Ibid., 25:23.

10. 1 Corinthians 12:4–7.

11. Ibid., 12:7.

12. GIRM, 111.

13. Ibid.

14. The Church, however, still treasures the wonderful body of music known as Gregorian chant, the ancient melodic patterns and absence of set meters require a completely different approach to singing. "The main place should be given, all things being equal, to Gregorian chant, as being proper to the Roman Liturgy. Other kinds of sacred music, in particular polyphony, are in no way excluded provided that they correspond to the spirit of the liturgical action and htat they foster the participation of al lthe faithful" (GIRM, 41).

Spirituality and Formation of the Cantor

As a cantor, you are a leader of liturgical prayer. To lead effectively, you will want to develop your own faith through good habits of prayer. There are many ways you can develop your spiritual life as a cantor.

The Liturgical Seasons

Become familiar with the liturgical calendar. Students and teachers learn the school calendar of classes, examinations, and vacation. Workers learn the company calendar of deadlines and holidays. Parents learn the family calendar of birthdays, sports schedules, and recitals. As a cantor, you become familiar with the liturgical calendar: seasons, and special days of the Lord, Mary, and the saints.

Easter falls on the Sunday following the first full moon of spring. There is always a full moon during Holy Week. The Sacred Paschal Triduum begins on Holy Thursday with the Evening Mass of the Lord's Supper and concludes after Evening Prayer on Easter Sunday. Those Three Days are the most important days of the Catholic calendar. They deserve full attention, preparation, and participation.

Lent begins on Ash Wednesday, six weeks before the Triduum. Easter Time concludes with the Solemnity of Pentecost, seven weeks after the Triduum.

Advent begins four Sundays before the Solemnity of the Nativity of the Lord (Christmas). It may or may not coincide with Thanksgiving weekend. Christmas Time ends with the Feast of the Baptism of the Lord, usually the third Sunday following the Solemnity of the Nativity of the Lord. However, if the Sunday on which the Solemnity of the Epiphany of the Lord is celebrated falls on January 7 or 8, the Feast of the Baptism of the Lord moves to the following day, a Monday.

The rest of the year is called Ordinary Time. It begins on the first weekday after the Feast of the Baptism of the Lord. That is why the first

Sunday that falls during Ordinary Time is called the Second Sunday of Ordinary Time. Ordinary Time is interrupted by Ash Wednesday and resumes after the Solemnity of Pentecost. The calendar is designed to end with the thirty-fourth week of Ordinary Time which is always the Solemnity of Our Lord Jesus Christ, King of the Universe. A week or two of Ordinary Time may vanish once Lent gets under way. Ordinary Time resumes after Pentecost with whichever week is necessary to end the liturgical year with the thirty-fourth week.

Celebrate the seasons. You probably decorate your home or office for Christmas. You may have Christmas sweatshirts, jewelry, or socks. Be mindful of the seasons all year round. Preserve a spirit of anticipation during Advent. Keep Christmas decorations up at home throughout the season—all the way to the Feast of the Baptism of the Lord.

Observe Lent. Make it a time for prayer, fasting, and almsgiving. Hold sacred the days of the Triduum. Avoid scheduling other events that conflict with a spirit of prayer on those days. Let the entirety of Easter Time resound with joy!

The Mass

Once you have made the liturgical calendar a part of your life, you will be better prepared to enter the spirit of the texts of the Mass. The Lectionary and *The Roman Missal* are arranged in ways to help you celebrate the seasons.

It is especially important to know the Sunday Lectionary. It is arranged over a three-year cycle of readings, featuring the Gospel according to Matthew, Mark, and Luke respectively. The Gospel according to John appears on many Sundays in Lent and Easter Time, as well as several summer Sundays in Year B and on the Second Sunday of Ordinary Time each year.

During Ordinary Time, the First Reading usually relates to the theme of the Gospel, and the Responsorial Psalm usually echoes the First Reading. For the Second Reading we hear excerpts from a New Testament letter; the same letter is heard for several weeks in a row.

Advent opens with readings about the Second Coming of Christ, and then it focuses on John the Baptist for the Second and Third Sundays. The Fourth Sunday of Advent tells part of the story leading up to the birth of Jesus in Bethlehem. Prophecies are announced in the First Readings throughout the season; the Second Reading looks forward to the coming of Christ.

During Lent, the First Readings tell the story of salvation history. The Second Readings tell of sin and repentance as they relate to other Scripture passages of the day. The Gospel for the First Sunday of Lent is always the temptation of Jesus in the desert. The Second Sunday tells of his Transfiguration. During Year A, the Gospel for the Third, Fourth, and Fifth Sundays fits well with the scrutinies of those preparing for Baptism during Easter. In the other years, the accounts of the Gospel tell stories of sin and death, together with the promise of forgiveness and Resurrection. The Sixth Sunday of Lent is Palm Sunday, the beginning of Holy Week. We always hear the Passion that day.

During Easter Time, the Gospel for the Second Sunday tells how the risen Christ appeared to the apostles on the Sunday after the Resurrection. The Gospel for the Third Sunday tells of Jesus breaking bread with the disciples after the Resurrection. The Gospel for the Fourth Sunday comes from the discourse of the Good Shepherd. The remaining Sundays put us at the Last Supper with Jesus while we hear his farewell discourse from John.

All of the other readings of Easter Time come from the New Testament: the Acts of the Apostles, in which we hear of the early Church; the first Letter of Peter, thought to be an extended homily on Baptism; the first Letter of John, with its encouragement of new Christians; and the Book of Revelation, which acclaims the risen Christ as the one deserving praise.

Especially if you are the psalmist, you will benefit by praying over the texts of any given Sunday. Start with the Gospel. Why was it chosen for this day? Move to the First Reading. Does it relate to the Gospel? Reflect on the Responsorial Psalm. How does it connect with the other readings so far? Pray over the Second Reading. What is its significance today?

During Ordinary Time, the Second Reading may have little to do with the other two. During Lent the First Reading relates to other First Readings of the season. It takes time to figure out why the readings were chosen, but it is not hard to do.

Focus on the Responsorial Psalm. Does the Lectionary present the entire psalm this week or only a few verses of one? If only a few verses, why were these particular verses chosen? Sometimes the answer is in the middle or end of the text. Examine the refrain. Does it come from the psalm? Or was it drawn from somewhere else? Sometimes the refrain comes from one of the other books of the Bible. Why was it chosen? Have the words been adapted? Sometimes the refrain is adapted so that it makes more sense on the lips of those who sing it today.

Once you have spent time with the readings, go another step with them. Get personal. Why did God inspire the sacred writers to compose these words? What do these texts have to say to you today? How is God addressing the situation in your life today? Is God asking something of you in these texts?

Now sing the psalm. You will discover it is more than words and notes. It is the Word of God. It will touch your heart, and your voice will communicate that message to the assembly of God's faithful ones.

Sacred Songs, Chants, and Hymns

The variety of sacred songs for Mass is endless. You may have a hymnal or other worship aid for the assembly's use. Get to know it well.

How is the hymnal arranged? Is the music organized by season of the year or alphabetically? Does it have a variety of settings of the parts of the Mass?

Examine the book for indexes. It probably has an alphabetical index, but it may have other ones as well. You may find an index of composers, for example, or an index of themes. Most interesting will be an index of Scripture passages to which the songs, chants, and hymns allude. If you look up the Lectionary citations for a particular Sunday, for example, you might find hymns that were written with one or more of the readings in mind. Study the text of those hymns. Do you see the connection? How has the author interpreted the biblical text?

Look at any one piece of music to learn additional information. Who is the composer? Who wrote the text? When was he or she born? Are the writers of this piece still alive? What do you know about them? Do you know anything about the circumstances that inspired them to compose these words and this music?

Do you understand the words? Sometimes the text is written in exquisite poetry. It takes a while to figure it out. Even a well-known hymn like "We Three Kings" raises questions. Does the first line mean "We are three kings from the Orient. Bearing gifts, we traverse afar"? Or does it mean "We three kings from the Orient are bearing gifts. We traverse afar"? The meaning does not change much, but it will change how you think about the words. Some people sing it as if "Orient Are" is the place from where the three kings come.

Spiritual Habits

Develop other spiritual habits. Sunday Mass is the most important hour of the week for Catholics. Is it a priority for you even when you are not the cantor? Do you prepare for Sunday Mass when you are not the singer?

Make *prayer* a part of your daily routine. To become fully imbued with the seasons and other observances during the liturgical year, the Liturgy of the Hours is an invaluable guide. Praying Morning and Evening Prayer every day develops sensitivity to the rhythms of the day and the turnings of the year. In the Liturgy of the Hours you will come to know the psalms. Many are selected to help you honor the time of the day. Others function as prophecies for the seasons of the year. The readings, antiphons, and intercessions all conspire to form a perfect background for Sunday worship.

Other *daily prayer* is beneficial. Many people enjoy taking time with the Bible, the Rosary, or a familiar prayer book. Some participate in daily Mass. Others visit the Blessed Sacrament for more extended periods of prayer and adoration. It is helpful to have a set time and a set place for your prayer. If you have a routine, you will find it easier to begin prayer each day, and its benefits will pervade your life.

Let the *Sacrament of Reconciliation* have an honored place in your spiritual life. As a cantor, you may be called on to sing at a communal Penance service at your church. Throughout the year you will lead the singing of music that cries out for God's mercy. If you are in touch with your own failures before the eyes of God, you will grow as God's child, and the sincerity of your belief will shine. You will meaningfully lead others through a penitential psalm, the hymns of Lent, and the Lamb of God because you have known the guilt of sin and the overpowering mercy of God.

Take advantage of *cantor workshops* offered in your area. Meet with cantors from other parishes. Exchange ideas, refine your abilities, and worship together as one.

Make time for a *retreat* at least once a year. Even if you cannot spend one or more nights at a retreat center, try to devote an entire day to prayer and reflection. Go somewhere special, some holy ground where others have met God. Keep the Triduum holy so you can fully immerse yourself into the meaning of the liturgies of Holy Week.

Musical Skills

Develop your musical skills. Meet with a voice instructor. Go to concerts. Listen to good recorded music. Hear how professionals sing and learn from them. Add your own gifts to what they can do—your gifts of faith, love, and service.

If you support the arts, they can reward your spiritual life. God is in the transcendentals: oneness, truth, and beauty. When you experience beauty, you are at God's threshold. Your spirit responds in ways beyond reason. You experience wonderment. That is the mysterious threshold that brings us to the presence of God.

As a singer, you experience that wonderment in the beauty of song. Your instrument is your very self. When you sing it is you who praises God—not you through an organ, a piano, a flute, or a guitar, but just you. God made you with a personality, a body, and a voice. You use it all to render praise.

When you develop your skills as a singer, your voice becomes more beautiful. It becomes the gateway that escorts others to the presence of God.

You might use the following prayer to prepare for your ministry:

Prayer of Preparation

God, the maker of all that is,
of all that can be seen,
of all that can be heard,
hear the prayer of your people,
and make our voices resound with your praise,
that they might please you
with words and melodies
that seek to show
the wonder that is you.
Through Christ our Lord.
Amen.

Questions for Discussion and Reflection

1. What are your responsibilities as a cantor? Are you a psalmist, a song leader, or a cantor?

   _____

   _____

   _____

   _____

2. What is your experience of God while you sing?

   _____

   _____

   _____

   _____

3. Why do you sing? When do you sing?

_____

_____

_____

_____

4. Whose singing do you enjoy? Why?

_____

_____

_____

_____

Serving as a Cantor

The Lord is worthy of all praise;
may he give you the gift of striving to sing a new song to him
with your voices, your hearts, and your lives,
so that one day you may sing that song for ever in heaven.

—*Book of Blessings, 1339*

Music, Liturgy, and the Cantor

Multiple Roles

Thus far in this book you have been invited to reflect on your ministry as a cantor and the role the cantor plays in communal worship. How to transfer these reflections into practical reality is not always easy to figure out: how do you respond to the call to lead the assembly's song and sung prayer, while at the same time remaining one with the people as a member of the assembly? How do you encourage the singing of the assembly without overpowering; empowering without dominating with your own voice? How can you be both present and transparent, letting the music serve the liturgy without becoming the focus? Being able to sing well is only the first step. As you know, the primary activity of the cantor goes far beyond mere music-making. Music is only the first layer of the ministry, the medium through which the ministry takes place.[1]

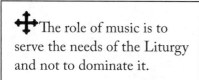

✙ The role of music is to serve the needs of the Liturgy and not to dominate it.

—*Sing to the Lord: Music in Divine Worship, 125*

A cantor should foster the "full, active and conscious participation" (CSL, 14) of the assembly.

Within the liturgy and its various sung moments, the cantor normally fills three distinct functions. At times you are the **song leader** or **animator,** whose job is to invite and support the song of the assembly. At times when the assembly needs vocal support, your job is simply to be present as a **member of the assembly** and model well

24

what everyone is asked to do in a given moment. Finally, during the Liturgy of the Word, you are called to be the **psalmist**, minister of the sung Word just as the lectors and readers are ministers of the spoken Word. As psalmist, your function is dual: You provide clear and hospitable leadership to the assembly, inviting and empowering their song. And, in the verses of the psalm, you do all you can to focus the assembly's attention on the text you are proclaiming, endeavoring to become transparent so the words of faith can shine through in all their splendor. Your role shifts from moment to moment, reaching into every moment of the liturgy from beginning to end.

> *At leadership moments, we want people to remember what we sang, so they can remember what they sang, so they can sing it again, and fall into the rhythm of the prayer.*
>
> *At moments of psalm or prayer proclamation, we want people to remember the words they heard, not the beauty of the song or of the singer. At moments when the people are secure enough in their own singing not to need us, we don't want them to remember that we were there at all.*

A Musical Journey through the Mass

Because the majority of cantors will serve primarily during Sunday Mass, it will be helpful to take a musical "walk" through the parts of the liturgy. There are four parts to the Mass: the Introductory Rites, the Liturgy of the Word, the Liturgy of the Eucharist, and the Concluding Rites. As a cantor, it is important to understand the progression of the liturgy with a particular focus on your role within it.

Introductory Rites

The Introductory Rites consist of the following:

- Entrance Procession and the Entrance Chant (or song)

- Sign of the Cross and Greeting

- Penitential Act and Kyrie—*or*—Rite of Blessing and Sprinkling of Water

- Gloria

- Collect

The purpose of the Introductory Rites is to help the assembled people "come together as one,"[2] preparing them for hearing God's Word and celebrating the Eucharist.

The Entrance Chant (Song)

The liturgy begins with a song, chant, or hymn with a fourfold purpose: It is intended to "open the celebration, foster the unity of those who have been gathered, introduce their thoughts to the mystery of the liturgical time or festivity, and accompany the procession of the Priest and ministers."[3] This musical selection is often in either strophic or verse-refrain form. The cantor should provide just enough guidance that the assembly feels secure in their singing but should be careful not to overpower them. The goal is to empower the people's song, providing needed support without drawing undue attention.

Sign of the Cross and the Greeting

After the Entrance Chant (Song), the priest makes the Sign of the Cross and greetings to the assembly, to signify "the presence of the Lord to the assembled community."[4] Both may be chanted by the priest. If chanted, the cantor may elicit the assembly's response.

Penitential Act and the Kyrie

During this rite, "the Priest calls upon the whole community to take part in the Penitential Act, which, after a brief pause for silence, it does by means of a formula of general confession."[5] Members of the assembly rejoice in God's mercy while silently recalling their sins.

There are three options for the Penitential Act. In the first option, the assembly prays the Confiteor together ("I confess to almighty God . . ."). The second option is a brief dialogue between the priest and the people. In each of these first two options, the words of absolution are then spoken or chanted by the priest, followed by the *Kyrie*.

The third option of the Penitential Act is slightly different, and it is this version which is most likely to involve the cantor. The text *Kyrie, eleison* ("Lord, have mercy"), is incorporated into a brief litany rather than concluding the text as in the first two options. The assembly is invited to respond after each of the three "tropes," expanded texts found in the Missal. In this option, the words of absolution follow the three tropes.

Rite of Blessing and Sprinkling of Water

Particularly during Easter Time, the Rite of Blessing and Sprinkling of Water may replace the Penitential Act and the Kyrie. Following the prayer of blessing over the water, the priest sprinkles the gathered faithful with the blessed water as a song or antiphon is sung. This song should be baptismal in nature. The cantor leads the singing here in whatever way would be most helpful to the assembly.

Gloria

The Gloria is "a very ancient and venerable hymn"[6] of praise to God that forms part of the "ordinary" of the Mass[7] and is to be sung during all Sunday liturgies except for those in the penitential seasons of Advent and Lent. The Gloria is also sung on solemnities and feasts. Settings of the Gloria are many and varied; some are in responsorial or song form, and others are through-composed; some are sung by the choir alone, some by everyone gathered together, and some by the choir or cantor in alternation with the assembly. How much leadership the cantor needs to give will depend entirely on the form of the musical setting used and the assembly's familiarity with the arrangement. As part of the ordinary of the Mass, it is best to have the assembly so comfortable with their part that the cantor is not needed at all.

The Collect

After a communal invitation to a brief, silent prayer, the Collect is prayed by the priest. The words of this prayer draw the attention of the assembly to the mysteries celebrated in a particular Mass. If the priest chants the Collect, the cantor may lead the assembly with the sung response, "Amen."

Liturgy of the Word

The Liturgy of the Word and the Liturgy of the Eucharist are the two primary parts of the Mass and are intimately connected.

In the Liturgy of the Word, Christ himself, the Word made flesh, is present in the proclamation of Scripture (both Old and New Testament). These ancient and holy texts are traditionally proclaimed from the ambo, the table of the Word—as the altar is the table of the Eucharist. This is where God speaks the truth of salvation to the gathered assembly.

The Liturgy of the Word includes the First Reading, Responsorial Psalm, Second Reading, the Gospel, Homily, Profession of Faith, and the Universal Prayer.

The Readings

✠ While the readings are ordinarily read in a clear, audible, and intelligent way, they may also be sung. "This singing, however, must serve to bring out the sense of the words, not obscure them."

—*Sing to the Lord: Music in Divine Worship, 153; referencing and quoting Lectionary for Mass, 14*

✠ Even if the readings are not sung, the concluding acclamation *The Word of the Lord* may be sung, even by someone other than the reader; all respond with the acclamation *Thanks be to God.* "In this way the assembled congregation pays reverence to the word of God it has listened to in faith and gratitude."

—*Sing to the Lord: Music in Divine Worship, 154; quoting Lectionary for Mass, 18*

Lectors and readers have the option of chanting the readings, provided the singing serves to bring out the sense and meaning of the words and does not cause them to get lost. In addition, or alternatively, they may chant "The Word of the Lord" and the conclusion to the readings, with the people responding, "Thanks be to God." Depending upon the musical skills of the lectors and readers, the parish staff may request that one who normally serves as cantor fulfill this role.

Responsorial Psalm

The psalm that follows the First Reading is "an integral part of the Liturgy of the Word" and "fosters meditation on the Word of God."[9] The Responsorial Psalm will be discussed in greater detail in the section of this book titled "The Cantor as Psalmist" on page 35.

The Responsorial Psalm is normally taken from the Book of Psalms, although at some points in the year a canticle (scriptural song) such as the *Magnificat* (Luke 1:46–55) or the Song of the Three Children (Daniel 3:23) will be indicated instead. The proper psalm for each day can be found in the Lectionary, which also gives options for seasonal psalms that may be substituted for the specified daily psalm.[10]

Because of the great importance of the psalm in the Liturgy of the Word, the psalm is normally sung from the ambo (or other appropriate place). The cantor normally intones the response, which the assembly repeats back. The cantor then proclaims the verses to the psalm, and the people respond to what they have heard by singing their response after each verse.

A Note about the "Responsorial" Psalm

Many people think that the term "responsorial" when applied to the psalm between the readings refers to the psalm's position as a "response" to the First Reading. In fact, while the psalms found in the Lectionary were indeed chosen to relate to the First Reading and Gospel of the day, the term "responsorial" refers not to the psalm's purpose but to its manner of singing. "Responsorial" singing, as far back as Gregorian chant and even beyond, is simply a dialogue form of singing between a cantor/ soloist and the larger group.

This can be confusing for some people—not only does it require for many of us a new way of thinking about the Responsorial Psalm, but we will encounter a great deal of music in the liturgy sung in a responsorial form: that is, alternating between assembly refrain and cantor verses.

Sequence

The sequence is a poetic, non-biblical chant sung on specified solemnities and feasts of the Church. Though at one time there were many sequences in use throughout the liturgical year, today they are observed on four specific instances. The Sequence is always to be sung on Easter Sunday (*Victimae paschali laudes*) and Pentecost Sunday (*Veni, Sancte Spiritus*), and the Easter sequence may be sung at Mass on each day of the Octave of Easter. The remaining two sequences, *Lauda Sion* and

Stabat Mater, may be sung on the Solemnity of the Host Holy Body and Blood of Christ and the memorial of Our Lady of Sorrows.

The sequence is sung immediately before the Gospel Acclamation. It can be sung by the cantor, choir, and/or assembly. Settings of the sequences are many; they are available from numerous publishers and found in most standard hymnals and worship resources.

Gospel Acclamation

In the acclamation before the Gospel, the assembly "welcomes and greets the Lord who is about to speak to them in the Gospel."[11] The response, intoned by the cantor and repeated by the congregation, is Alleluia during most of the year and is replaced by another response (or omitted) during the Lenten season. The cantor then sings the Gospel verse specified for that liturgy, and the assembly repeats their response. This acclamation usually accompanies the procession with the *Book of the Gospels*.

Gospel

Like the First and Second Readings, a priest or deacon who is comfortable singing may choose to chant the Gospel text. As an alternative, he may sing only the invitation ("The Lord be with you" and "A reading from the holy Gospel according to . . .") and the conclusion ("The Gospel of the Lord"). In each of these cases, the cantor may assist the assembly on their responses as needed. On Palm Sunday and Good Friday, if the Passion is chanted, the cantor may be called upon to participate in the chanting of the Passion, which is often carried out by multiple voices.

Profession of Faith

The singing of the Creed (Apostles' or Nicene) is to be sung or said on Sundays and solemnities,[12] but generally this communal Profession of Faith is recited by all. The cantor alone or with the choir can be of great assistance to congregations for whom singing the Creed is new. Once the assembly has become accustomed to singing this part of the Mass, there may not be a need for the cantor.

Universal Prayer

In the Universal Prayer (or Prayer of the Faithful), the people of God gather their prayers on behalf of the Church, the world, the oppressed, and the local community. When these prayers are sung, the cantor chants the prayer of petition and invites the assembly to join in the response, usually "Lord, hear our prayer" or some similar text. The Prayer of the Faithful concludes the Liturgy of the Word.

Liturgy of the Eucharist

In the Liturgy of the Eucharist, the assembled faithful prepare to celebrate the central rite of our faith: Communion with Jesus Christ in the transformed elements of bread and wine, sharing in the Paschal Mystery through his Body and Blood. The Liturgy of the Eucharist begins with the Preparation of the Gifts, continues with the Eucharistic Prayer, and concludes with the Communion Rite (Lord's Prayer, Sign of Peace, Lamb of God, reception of Holy Communion, and Prayer after Communion).

Offertory Chant (Song)

The Liturgy of the Eucharist begins with the Preparation of the Gifts. The collection is taken up, the altar is prepared for Communion, and members of the liturgical assembly bring forward the gifts of bread and wine. The Offertory Chant or Song, sung at this time, can be in almost any musical form and may be sung by cantor, choir, and/or assembly.

Preface Dialogue

The Preface dialogue begins the Eucharistic Prayer. If the priest celebrant chooses to chant the Preface dialogue, the cantor may lead the people in singing their responses. As with all such moments, it is the cantor's job to lead these responses only as necessary to facilitate the people's singing, without dominating the sound.

Eucharistic Prayer and Acclamations

The Eucharistic Prayer is the "center and high point"[13] of the entire liturgical celebration. In this prayer, the gifts of bread and wine are sanctified, made holy, and transformed into the Body and Blood of

Christ. Though there are several options for the Eucharistic Prayer, they all have essentially the same components: praise and thanksgiving, the Institution narrative (the re-telling of the Last Supper and Christ's command to eat and drink of his Body and Blood); the anamnesis (making present the past and anticipating the future); the epiclesis (the calling down of the Holy Spirit on the gifts); and prayers of intercession for the whole Church.

This lengthy prayer, extending from the Preface Dialogue all the way through to the Amen at its conclusion, should be treated as the single ritual event that it is. The prayer itself may be sung by the priest in part or throughout. The cantor will usually take an active role in leading the ordinary acclamations of the Eucharistic Prayer: the Holy, Holy, Holy; the Memorial Acclamation; and Amen. These acclamations are usually unified by the musical setting, and most parishes will only have a few sets of acclamations rotating throughout the liturgical year. Once a set of acclamations is comfortable and set in the voices of the assembly, the cantor may be able to step back entirely from the microphone at these moments and allow the singing to belong entirely to the people.

The following cues will be helpful for cantors unsure of when and what acclamations to sing:

HOLY, HOLY, HOLY *(SANCTUS)*: This is sung following the Preface to the Eucharistic Prayer and is an acclamation of praise and thanksgiving. Cantors should listen for the concluding phrase to the Preface, which always emphasizes our belief that our prayer is joined with the hymns of the angels and saints.

MEMORIAL ACCLAMATION: The Memorial Acclamation follows the words of institution in the Eucharistic Prayer and transitions the prayer into the anamnesis, the memorial of Christ's Death and Resurrection and the belief that in these actions the act of salvation becomes present in the here and now. In this acclamation, the cantor will lead the assembly in one of three acclamations:

- "We proclaim your Death, O Lord, and profess your Resurrection until you come again."

- "When we eat this Bread and drink this Cup, we proclaim your death, O Lord, until you come again."

- "Save us, Savior of the world, for by your Cross and Resurrection you have set us free."

AMEN: At the conclusion of the Eucharistic Prayer, the priest sings (or says) what is called the final doxology: "Through him, and with him, and in him, / O God, almighty Father, in the unity of the Holy Spirit, / all honor and glory is yours, / for ever and ever." The assembly responds with an "Amen." The cantor may lead this as well.

Please see page 48 regarding posture and other reflections regarding the cantor's role during the Eucharistic Prayer.

Lord's Prayer

The Lord's Prayer may be sung. Whether in the traditional chant version or a more contemporary setting, it is especially important that the cantor's leadership, if it is needed at all, does not impede the ability of the people to participate fully.

Lamb of God (Agnus Dei)

The Lamb of God or *Agnus Dei* is a litany accompanying the breaking of the Eucharistic bread by the priest. Normally it is a threefold litany, although it can be extended as needed to cover the ritual action in cases where more faithful are gathered and more Extraordinary Ministers and vessels are needed. The litany will always conclude with "Grant us peace."

Communion Chant (Song)

The rites of the Church are clear that the Communion Song is intended to be a moment for the entire assembly to sing together; however, there are provisions for a choir-only piece at this time. This moment, perhaps more than any other in the liturgy, presents a particular challenge for the cantor. During the Communion procession, people are walking, receiving Holy Communion, returning to their places, and praying; asking them to sing as well is asking a lot. There is a delicate balance to be found here for the cantor. On the one hand, if a song for the assembly is chosen, it is important that you continue to use your best skills in leading and empowering the assembly to find its voice. On the other, if the reality in your parish is that very few people choose to sing this piece, it's important that your audible and prayerful presence in the microphone be at least enough that those who would like to sing are able to do so.

The processional nature of the ritual moment means that strophic hymnody (with its many words and no repetition) is often not the best choice for the Communion song. Verse-refrain music can work very well; if sung responsorially, with the cantor singing the verses and the assembly singing the refrain. An easily memorized refrain or repeated section of music is most appropriate to accompany a procession, although, if desired, the people may of course be invited to join in singing the verses. As with the Entrance Chant, *The Roman Missal* specifies a set of Communion Antiphons for people to sing, a few settings of which are currently available. Please refer to the resources list on page 69.

Song of Praise

Following the distribution of Holy Communion and the silent prayer which follows it,[14] the liturgical documents provide the option of inviting the assembly to sing a song of praise. While this option is not exercised in many communities as yet, the tradition is growing slowly as parishes discover how effective a communal song of thanksgiving after Holy Communion can be for reaffirming the unity and oneness of the community after our individual receptions of the sacrament and the private prayer that follows.[15]

Prayer after Communion

The Prayer after Communion concludes the Liturgy of the Eucharist. Like the Collect, it may be chanted by the priest celebrant. If chanted, the cantor may lead the assembly's, "Amen."

Concluding Rite

The Concluding Rite begins following the Prayer after Communion. At this time, announcements are heard and the Final Blessing is given. The assembly, transformed by the Word they have heard and the Eucharist they have received, is dismissed and sent into the world to glorify God by their lives.

The Final Greeting, Blessing, and Dismissal

The priest may chant the Final Greeting, Blessing, and Dismissal. The blessing may be in a simple form or the more solemn threefold blessing. The cantor may lead the necessary sung responses, especially if the assembly is unfamiliar with or new to this practice.

Closing or Recessional Song

Although it is common practice in the United States to conclude the Mass with a closing song and acknowledged as such in *Sing to the Lord: Music in Divine Worship*, it is interesting to note that the *General Instruction of the Roman Missal* makes no mention of such a song. *Sing to the Lord* also suggests that if a congregational song was sung after Communion, an instrumental piece might be more appropriate.[16]

The Cantor as Psalmist

Even older than the liturgy itself are the Scripture texts from the Book of Psalms. These ancient songs were already deeply imbued in the hearts and tasted on the lips of God's people when Jesus of Nazarath walked among us. He learned and sang and prayed them through his life, as do we today. They form an unshakable bond between our ancestors and us—an intimacy of experience and emotion matched by no other body of texts. For while all of Scripture is holy and inspired by God, the psalms carry forward the hopes and fears and emotions of the people who lived the stories. Think of each psalm not as simply a piece of Scripture (although of course it is), but as the experience of a single individual at a particular moment in time—a real person, who lived and breathed and hurt and celebrated and wept and laughed. Every single human emotion known to our lovely and fallen race is expressed some-where in these 150 poetic songs: rejoicing, thanksgiving, praise, sorrow, lament, anger, fear, trust, and so many more. A story—a recounting of events—can be told in words. When the emotion is too great for a sim-ple narrative to carry, we have to sing.

The Presence of the Psalmist

Normally, the Responsorial Psalm should be proclaimed from the ambo—the same place from which the readings are proclaimed. While it is also acceptable to proclaim the Responsorial Psalm from another location, doing so blurs the already somewhat nebulous distinction between the Responsorial Psalm and the other parts of the liturgy led by the cantor. Always remember that, when you are filling the ministry of psalmist, you are doing something completely different from all other parts of your ministry.[17]

Therefore, before you even look at the actual psalm itself, be aware of your presence when proclaiming it. However hard you work to achieve invisibility and unobtrusiveness in other liturgical moments, at this moment you are to be entirely visible and command the focus of the room. And yet, once you have that focus, your job is to redirect it, and let it rest upon the words you sing. Remember, your goal here is for people to remember what you sang, not how beautifully you sang it. There is no concrete way to explain how to do this, except to stress yet again that complete confidence and security in your words and music is the imperative first step.

It is then your task to enter into that proclamation yourself, hearing it in your own heart and letting it shine forth in all the clarity and vulnerability of the first psalmist who uttered the same words thousands of years ago. It should also be noted that if true "responsorial" singing is intended as a dialogue between psalmist and assembly, then ideally you should not need to sing on the people's response at all. This is a twofold challenge. On the one hand, especially for those parishes that use the proper psalm of the week each Sunday, it may take an assembly more than one hearing to grasp a psalm text and melody. When this is the case, you as cantor are operating under a bit of a "split-personality." During the verses you are psalmist, and during the response you are song leader or animator. When there is a choir present during the liturgy, some of this tension is relieved; the choir can support the assembly on the responses,

During the verses of the psalm, the cantor serves as psalmist, and during the response the cantor is a song leader or animator.

freeing you to simply be psalmist. If it hasn't been a parish's practice to sing the Responsorial Psalm, beginning with the seasonal psalms provided in the Lectionary can help the assembly become familiar with singing the psalms.

The second challenge here is one of unfamiliarity: Most cantors have never had the experience of standing at an ambo before hundreds of people, looking at them, and not singing. Most cantors, even knowing that their sung support is not needed, cannot resist singing with the people's part, not because the people need it but because the sense of self-consciousness and exposure in standing silent and receiving the assembly's response is too much to bear. But try! Remember that the psalm is a dialogue, and to dialogue one must speak and then be silent, listening for the response of the other, before speaking again.

> *As always, consult with your music director before attempting to make changes in your ministry. For some parishes, the Gospel Acclamation is a safer and less threatening place to start acclimating cantors and assemblies to this true dialogue form, before trying it with the psalm.*

The Cantor as Minister of the Word

Many cantors, when doing their preparation for liturgy, make the mistake of treating the Responsorial Psalm like just another song in the list of music they need to learn. This could not be further from the truth; the psalm is the central moment of the cantor's liturgical ministry, and it must be treated as such. Here, you are not simply a music minister or a minister of hospitality as you are when you lead song. You are a minister of the Word, the keeper and holder of the sung Scriptures for the community.

Musical settings of the psalms generally fall into two major categories: chant-tone psalmody and metric psalmody.[18] Singers are generally more comfortable with metric psalmody (in basic "song form," with melody and rhythm fully composed through refrain and verses). The danger here is that it takes at least twice the skill in

> ✠ The psalmist, or cantor of the Psalm, sings the Psalm verses at the ambo or another suitable place.
>
> —*General Instruction of the Roman Missal*, 61

> *"When it happens to me to be more moved by the singing than by what is sung, I confess myself to have sinned criminally, and then I would have rather not heard the singing at all."*
>
> —*St. Augustine*

such a setting to make the words reign supreme and be remembered above a pretty melodic setting. In the words of St. Augustine, "When it happens to me to be more moved by the singing than by what is sung, I confess myself to have sinned criminally, and then I would have rather not heard the singing at all."[19] For this reason, more and more parishes are shifting to chanted psalmody, with a melodic refrain and a chant tone for the verses; the style is clearly distinguished from all the other singing at liturgy, and it is simple and stark enough that the text can more easily be heard and taken in.

The automatic reaction of most cantors, especially those who read music, is to pick up the music and simply sing the phrase. This is not the best approach! Remember that in this moment you are first and foremost a minister of the Word, so do what a minister of the Word would do here: Start with the text. The first few times through the psalm verses do not sing them or put them to music. Speak through them out loud (not just silently in your head). Read them the way a lector or reader would read them, and repeat them this way until they are comfortable on your lips and the meaning and intent is clear in your mind.

Only then should you move to singing, but not yet to singing the tone as written. Take an intermediate step and try chanting the words on a single pitch, with the same speed and inflection you used when you spoke. Most people think of speech and song as radically different things. In the ancient Church, however, they were much more closely related. In fact, in ancient Hebrew and Greek there was not even a separate word for "music."[20] Speech was speech until it crossed over into the area of poetry and chanting and took on musical qualities. The intermediate step of single-pitch chanting the spoken texts can help blur the distinction a little and achieve the speech-song quality of chant for which you are striving. Like the spoken text exercise, practice this one also until you can do it comfortably and without "bumps" in the chant. Only then (after making sure you are comfortable with the chant tone's melody line) should you attempt to marry the text with the psalm tone, still keeping the text moving at speech-rhythm and with the inflections and pacing of the spoken word as much as possible. By this point, you should be able not only to chant these texts clearly and with confidence (with the text as your main focus), but you've also engaged in enough repetition that you should be able to move beyond the notes and words on the page into the area of truly praying the texts. This may seem like a lengthy process, but it does not take as long as it sounds, and it is worth every minute.

The Cantor as Musician

Until this point, this book has looked primarily at the non-musical aspects of being a cantor. It should go without saying that there must be a solid base of musicianship at the core of your ministry, or nothing can be accomplished. This base must be secure enough and your preparation extensive enough that you can be attentive to the other aspects of your ministry, and to those to whom you minister.

Training

Before everything else, a cantor should have a pleasant voice and the ability to use it to its best advantage.[21] You should be able to sing in tune, in the range required of the music (usually quite modest since most

> *"Well trained" and "well prepared" do not mean that a cantor must be formally trained. A good cantor should have a pleasant voice, be able to sing in tune, and exhibit prayerful and hospitable leadership skills.*

of the cantor's repertoire is in the same range asked of the assembly), and with enough clarity of pronunciation and vocal strength to proclaim the text well. While for some this comes naturally (or more likely has been a part of a person's life since childhood), for others additional study may be needed. Most parish music directors or music ministers, if they are not able to provide assistance themselves, are happy to recommend voice teachers or workshops for their cantors to work on their vocal techniques; the music departments of local colleges or even high schools can often help a singer locate a good teacher.

The ability to read music is also valuable; any cantor who has not had the chance to learn in the past should pursue it at first opportunity. The ability to acquire a piece of music on your own fosters independence and confidence, and saves a tremendous amount of time and work when learning a piece of music. It cannot be said more plainly than this: If you cannot read music, it is worth your time to learn. That said, not being able to read music does not necessarily exclude you from cantor ministry. If you can't read music, but have a good ear, you will need to allow for extra rehearsal time when learning new music. Recordings of published liturgical music are increasingly available and can make the process easier, or you can record cantor rehearsals or choir practices for later study. Please note that recordings can be equally valuable tools for those who do read music; they can give a sense of the character and style of a particular piece and help you grow more comfortable with how your part works with the accompaniment instrument.

Preparations for the Cantor

Anyone who has ever served as a cantor knows the many layers of work involved in the preparation and execution of this ministry. This section of the book will examine the physical, mental, and spiritual preparation involved in serving as a cantor.

Care of the Human Voice

Suggestions for Healthy Singing

1. *Eat a balanced diet.*

2. *Avoid caffeine, refined sugar and starches, and alcohol.*

3. *Keep physically fit.*

4. *Avoid stress.*

5. *Drink lots of water.*

6. *Warm up.*

Of all musicians, singers are the ones whose instrument is a part of the body and not an external contraption of metal or wood. Any instrument needs good care and regular preventative maintenance; the vocal instrument is no exception. Complicating this issue is the reality that we cannot easily examine the inner workings of the instrument for stress or damage; all we can do is evaluate based on how we feel at any given moment. Medications to treat bodily illness, effective as they may be for their intended purpose, sometimes have a negative effect on the voice itself. Therefore, preventative maintenance is by far the best route to pursue—take care of your body, head to toe, and your vocal instrument will in most cases take care of itself. You have doubtless heard it before, many times: Eat a sensible and balanced diet, and avoid excessive caffeine, refined sugars and starches, and alcohol. Exercise regularly. Get plenty of rest. Avoid stress. Mental and emotional anxieties have profound and immediate effects on the body in general and tend to manifest very quickly in the voice and throat. Be aware of how you use your voice in non-singing situations. The best vocal singing technique can be completely undone by abuse of the vocal cords and poor vocal speaking technique. Above all, stay well hydrated, all the time, not just when you are singing. It cannot be stressed too much: You cannot care for your voice without caring for your whole self.

We will look at some simple warm-up and vocal health issues starting on page 42–46, and other suggested resources are given on page 69. Still, vocal technique is a complex issue and one the learning of which cannot and should not be attempted from a book; it is always best to work with choral directors or teachers.

Warming Up

If you were to get into your car on a cold February morning, back out of the garage, and immediately pull onto the expressway at 60 miles per hour, you would probably not be surprised to find that your automobile did not perform as well as it should. Nor would an athlete simply leap out of bed in the morning, swallow a quick cup of coffee, and immediately run a marathon. Yet far too many singers attempt the exact vocal parallel to these situations on Sunday mornings, especially at an early morning liturgy. You owe it to your instrument (and yourself) to prepare your voice for the work it needs to do, if you are to do it well and without doing damage to your instrument.

Many singers are reliant on a bottle of water beside them at all times while singing; often this reliance is due to the fact that they do not hydrate consistently, all the time, 24/7. Consistent and steady hydration should correct the need to sip water after every song, even in very dry spaces.

See pages 42–46 for examples of simple vocal warm-ups. While each person will have their own approach to warm-ups, the basic components will usually be the same: stretching, breath work, basic phonation, low-range singing, high-range singing, and mobility of enunciators.

STRETCHING: Stretch both arms over your head. Reach up very slowly with one arm at a time, as though you were climbing a rope ladder; feel the stretch down your sides all the way to your waist. From the same position, slowly reach your left arm sideways over your head to your right, as though making the "C" from the well-known "YMCA" dance. Hold this stretch for a few moments, and then return to center.

> *Obviously, do these stretches only to the extent you are physically able to do so, and stop if you feel any pain. Pain is your body telling you you're trying to do more than it's able to do; listen to it!*

Repeat to the left. Gently shake out your arms and shoulders.

Drop your arms to your sides and slowly roll your shoulders: Take them forward, then up, then back, then down. Repeat this motion a few times, and then reverse. Drop your head down to the front (just your head; keep your shoulders comfortably upright and relaxed). Let your head roll gently to the side until your right ear is over your right shoulder, being careful not to raise the shoulders. Feel the gentle stretch down the left side of your neck. Let your head roll back to center front, and then repeat the stretch to your left, so that you feel the stretch down the right side of your neck. Repeat this back and forth several times. End with the head dropped to the front; inhale slowly, lifting your head as you breathe, and then exhale, staying upright.

> *Some people prefer to do these head rolls all the way around, first to the right, then to the back, then left, and finally forward once again. However, this can cause significant discomfort to the back of the neck if not done properly, and the stretch to the back does not accomplish much more than the simple back and forth front stretch.*

Take a few minutes to gently massage your facial muscles, concentrating especially on the cheeks and jaw. Stretch and scrunch your whole face a few times, to open up and release any lingering tension in these muscles. A gentle neck-and-back rub (self-administered can do a wonderful job if there is no one to assist!) to the neck and upper shoulders can work wonders for releasing tension to the face and head.

BREATH WORK: The muscles of the rib cage and back, which primarily assist our breathing, also should be gently worked into action. Breathe deeply, either through the nose alone or through the nose and mouth together, feeling the breath fill your ribcage and expand it all the way down to your waist, and then slowly exhale. Do this several times. (For many experienced singers, this deep breathing can be combined with the physical stretching exercises, in which each enhances the other and a small amount of time is saved.)

BASIC PHONATION: Most singers, before moving into specific vocal warm-ups, will engage in some very simple and basic phonation, depending on their voice type. A series of gentle hum, sighs or "siren" sounds on a neutral "ooh" or "oh" vowel help to awaken the vocal cords and get them moving.

LOW-RANGE SINGING: Having access to a piano or keyboard is helpful for these exercises. Simple note patterns (such as the one below), sung each time lowered by a half-step, help to awaken the lower registers:

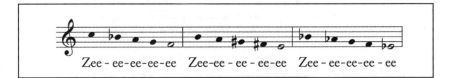

Proceed down by half-steps, in a gentle neutral volume (do not over-sing, especially when waking and warming the voice), as far as your voice is comfortable; try to stretch your range a little as time goes by, but don't overdo! It also can help to vary the vowels you sing; generally when singing lower, it is easier to use the "brighter" vowels, such as "eeh" or "eh." Once you're well warmed up on an "eeh" vowel, try challenging yourself by singing the same exercise on an "aah" vowel, or in alternation.

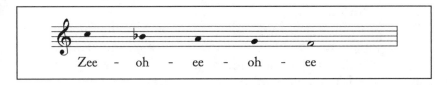

HIGH-RANGE SINGING: Just like the low-range warm-ups, singing some simple patterns on different vowels, ascending by half-steps, can be a good way to awaken the higher registers of the voice.

Below are some examples of good warm-ups to take you into the higher registers, with suggestions for different vowels to try. There are, of course, endless possibilities here. Use your imagination and see what works best for you.

As with the low-range exercises, while we do want to challenge ourselves to expand our range over time, we should not overdo. Singing to the point of pain or uncomfortable tension is never a good idea, and in warm-ups it is especially counterproductive.

MOBILITY OF ENUNCIATORS: These last sets of exercises are designed to get the "enunciators" moving—those parts of our mouths which enable us to proclaim text clearly (diction). Our lips, tongues, cheeks, and jaws are as sluggish as any part of us early in the morning, and they need gentle waking up as well. Again, there are countless options: Some singers will choose a particular passage of poetry ("Jabberwocky" by Lewis Carroll is a mouth-twisting favorite) or song ("Modern Major General" from *Pirates of Penzance*, or the final countdown of "The Twelve Days of Christmas," for example). Any of a hundred children's rhymes or tongue-twisters can serve, as long as the mouth gets moving!

Learning Your Music

This should go without saying, but it is imperative that cantors know their music inside and out. This is the "mental" part of our "physical-mental-spiritual" preparation. You should rehearse or review every piece of music in the liturgy before standing up to sing, even if you think you are familiar with the song, hymn, or chant. Sometimes a familiar tune will have a different text; sometimes the text underlay of verse 3 may be different from verse 2; sometimes a hymn may be in a higher key than you are accustomed to singing; sometimes a song you know very well may not have crossed your lips in a year or two. This is twice as important for new music—if a piece is unfamiliar, sufficient time must be given to its learning that the cantor can sing it, not just accurately, but with complete confidence and assurance in order to lead and sustain the singing of the assembly.

Do not simply mentally scan through the texts and music you are going to sing; it is crucial that you physically sing through the music you are preparing. Researchers have long been aware of the concept of "muscle memory" in repeated activities—neural pathways created by repetition, that make the action easier to repeat; the more repetition, the stronger the pathways. Even if it is difficult to find an opportunity, it is important that a singer find a place and time to rehearse full voice,[22] without feeling the need to hold back.

Unless the words, pitches, and rhythms of the music you are singing are absolutely well-known and familiar to you, it will be impossible to free yourself from the music and engage the other layers of this important and substantial ministry.

Music Outside of the Liturgy

It's easy to get so involved in life as a liturgical music minister that we forget how to simply enjoy good music, of whatever kind. Make sure, as you work at being the best cantor you can possibly be, to remember that the best cantor will always be someone who loves music. Enjoy your ministry, yes, but broaden your musical horizons to enjoy different genres and styles of music. If you love classical symphonic music, get tickets to hear the symphony, but also open your mind and heart by listening to a jazz radio station, downloading an MP3 of West African traditional drumming, or going salsa dancing. If you dare, borrow your teenager's MP3 player and try to enter into it. The best way to understand any cultural or age group is by learning to understand its music. Keep your experience as a lover of music alive and well, and you will never burn out or lose your sense of wonder as a minister of music.

The Cantor as Song Leader or Animator

When you think of the cantor's ministry, the image of the song leader or "animator" is probably the first one that comes to mind. The "how" of the animator role is not a single event, but a process that develops over time. The process is a dynamic one, taking into account the assembly present in any given parish at any given moment. There is no one correct way to lead an assembly in song. Your responsibility is to learn and know your assembly the same way you learn and know your music, and to nurture the musical instrument that is their voice with the same care you give your own. In this, you are truly more a "minister of hospitality" than simply a music minister. You are there to offer gracious assistance and comfort to those whom you serve, and to help them feel not just warmly welcomed but truly at home in the liturgy.

Facial Expressions and Gestures

While many of the factors which will decide whether an assembly decides to sing the liturgy are outside of your control, one factor is entirely up to you: your own face and persona as you sing and lead. It is your manner that will help people feel welcomed and empowered to sing the liturgy. If you can consistently approach your public ministry with warmth, openness, accessibility, and confidence, and let these be seen on your face, people will not be able to help but respond over time.

Once your smiling face and warm, confident voice have engaged people's willingness to sing, your remaining major work in the song leader's or animator's role centers around the gestures you use to encourage and empower assembly singing. The repertoire of gestures a cantor uses is wide and will depend at every turn on a series of variables:

1. **Musical concerns:** What is the musical form of the piece of music? Do the people sing throughout, or only on refrains, or is the song a call-and-response dialogue between the cantor and the assembly?

2. **Hospitality concerns:** How well does the assembly know this piece? What is the "personality" of the assembly at a particular time of day? Does this assembly sing comfortably on their own, or do they rely heavily on the guidance of the musical leadership?

3. **Spatial concerns:** How big is the worship space? How big is the assembly? How tall is the cantor? Where is the cantor located in relationship to the rest of the assembly? Is the cantor positioned in a place of leadership?

4. **Microphone and stand concerns:** How live is the sound system, and how close to the microphone does the cantor need to be to achieve optimal (but not overbearing) amplification? (Bear in mind that the

A one-armed gesture is appropriate in small spaces or where the music is familiar.

answer will be different for every cantor, as each person's personal vocal quality, microphones, and church acoustics will determine this factor!) Is the placement of the microphone such that consonants are carried clearly, without loud popping on "p" or other explosive consonant sounds?[23] Is the music stand at an appropriate height for reading the music, or does the cantor need to hold the music in hand in order to see it clearly, and what can be done to address this? Is the arrangement of microphone, stand, and music such that a cantor can safely gesture and turn pages without bumping music or microphones?

These are just a start. The more you start paying attention to nuances, the longer this list of variables becomes, and the more your gestures and presence to the assembly will reflect each individual group. The basic gesture will look something like this: On the last beat or two before you are to enter singing, as you inhale, let your intake of breath be the impetus to raise your arms in a gentle curve similar

> *Gesturing Rule #1: The gesture happens before you sing; the assembly should not just be able to sing with you, they should be able to breathe with you.*

to the orans posture used by the priest celebrant at many moments in the liturgy—arms raised and extended to the sides, a little over the head. On the first beat you sing, let the hands extend a bit, as you bring the people in. The height of the arms will depend both on the size of the room and the size of the cantor. A tall cantor singing in a small space may only need to bring the arms up to shoulder level in a gesture similar to inviting someone forward for a hug. A petite cantor in a larger room will probably need to raise the arms much higher into almost a "V" shape in order to be seen. In smaller worship spaces, or in groups where the music is quite familiar, a one-armed gesture may be perfectly sufficient. On music that is especially well-known within a more intimate assembly, the gesture can sometimes be accomplished simply with one's facial

In some spaces, both arms are needed when gesturing.

features: a lift of the head and a moment of inviting eye contact. The important factor to remember with a gesture of any size is that it must come enough before the singing that the people have time to breathe: Remember that you're not just inviting them to sing with you, you're inviting them to breathe with you first. This is the only absolute; almost everything else about a cantor's gesture—when, how big, how often—will relate directly to your ability to respond to what you hear from your assembly. Consult with your parish music director; experiment a little. If you pay attention to your own gestures, you will soon figure out what works best for you and elicits the best response from the people.

Always listen to the voice of your assembly.

Listening to the Assembly's Voice

Listening to the assembly is perhaps the most difficult aspect of being a cantor for us to master, and yet it is probably the most important. The ability to listen and respond to our assemblies, taking nothing for granted, reacting to what we are hearing moment to moment, and tailoring our response to it, is absolutely central to our ministry. This skill is very difficult to explain or teach from a text, and it takes years to hone.

First and foremost, although it has been said before, it is crucial that cantors be absolutely solid on the notes, words, and rhythms of the music they are singing. Without utter assurance from their leader, not only will people not get the support they need and deserve, but they may give up all together. If the cantor cannot manage a song, they are likely to think, there is no way they can expect to do it. Without complete confidence in your own words and music, it is extremely difficult to move beyond yourself into a true listening connection with the assembly.

Different musical forms will also affect our gestures. In a strophic hymn, the assembly may need a good strong gesture to get them started at the beginning of the hymn; on the other hand, if

> **Gesturing Rule #2:** *Only gesture when you believe the gesture will accomplish something. If the people do not need your gesture to facilitate their singing, then don't gesture!*

your space has a good instrument and the hymn is very familiar, the gesture may not be needed. With a verse-refrain piece of music, some assemblies will need a gesture at the beginning of each verse and each refrain; others will not. (In this case, at least a facial acknowledgment of the assembly's entrance on each part of the song is helpful, unless one is working in a space so large that even a prominent face-and-head gesture will not be seen.)

A responsorially sung piece of music will definitely need a gesture at each assembly refrain. As a general rule, whenever the status quo changes (for example, solo singing gives way to assembly singing), a gesture is definitely called for. Litanies will behave the same way, the only exception being that in a very long litany (the Litany of the Saints, for example, or a long and familiar litany for the Prayer of the Faithful) the cantor may be able to diminish or eliminate the gesture altogether by the end. Only gesture when the gesture will make a difference. If it is not needed, don't gesture!

Then how do we know when a gesture is needed? How do we know when to back off from the microphone and when to stay present? Oddly, this question is not as difficult to answer as it sounds, and most cantors are able (when they get beyond their own difficulties with the music and texts) to answer it relatively easily—once they get into the habit of asking it of themselves. It is a question that needs to be asked, not just once in a liturgy, but literally dozens or even hundreds of times.

As you make your gesture at the beginning of a familiar verse-refrain hymn at the Preparation of the Gifts, for example, scan the room to see how many people have their hymnals or worship aids out and are ready to sing. See how many truly are breathing with you. As you begin singing, listen carefully to discern whether you can hear the voice of the assembly singing with you. If you can clearly hear them, try backing off slightly from the microphone. After a few measures, listen carefully again. Did your movement away from the microphone cause the assembly's voice to strengthen or weaken? If the latter is the case, then subtly move back to the microphone and remain clearly audible through the remainder of the verse. Listen

Naturally, the decision of how and when a cantor should move away from the microphone should be made in conversation with the music director of your parish; especially in communities with multiple cantors, consistency is very important.

again when you reach the refrain, which is typically the part of the song that an assembly is most comfortable with. Can you hear them singing? If so, back off slightly from the microphone. Some assemblies sing better with firm support from a cantor, and others are more likely to rally forth with strength when the cantor moves back from the microphone. The only way to discover which of these you are ministering to on a given Sunday is to pay attention and learn.

This constant adjusting-readjusting process can be exhausting at first, but it eventually becomes automatic and is the sign of a truly excellent cantor.

The Cantor as Model

It sounds a bit strange to say, but our goal as cantor in almost all song leader or animator moments should be, over time, to render ourselves obsolete. Our role is to lead, but in a leadership which consistently defers to the primary choir of the liturgy, the gathered assembly. Over time, if your parish's cantors habituate themselves in the processes outlined above, you will notice that you are able to move farther and farther from the microphones for longer spaces of time (especially in the ordinary of the Mass). If you are in a parish where this is already the case, bravo! This is a powerful opportunity. When the assembly's voice becomes strong enough that you are not needed for entire sung portions of the liturgy, instead of moving to the microphone for the *Sanctus*, remain in your place a few feet away from the microphone and give a gesture just large enough that the people can see that you are cuing them in—perhaps simply a facial one. Think of the message you com-

municate in that moment, when you acknowledge that no leadership is needed and you choose to sing simply as a member of the assembly. And think of what is further communicated a few weeks later when even that small gesture can disappear and the assembly is completely on their own, confident in the strength of their voices. Moments such as these are the "Holy Grail" of cantors and should be sought after and cultivated as much as possible.

The cantor's goal is to lead the gathered assembly with sung prayer.

The Cantor's Life of Prayer

Your children have the flu and the baby was up all night teething, you had a disagreement with our spouse or parent in the morning, and your boss at work has been out of sorts all week. And now it is time to go to church and serve as cantor for liturgy, leading several hundred people in song and praise. You don't even have the luxury of showing up and just singing, because if you don't enter into the prayer and allow yourself to be connected to your brothers and sisters in faith, you can't really say that you're fulfilling your ministry in the liturgical celebration. How can you manage this? How do you make yourself transparent enough to serve in this way, especially on the days it was all you could manage just to show up?

Between your warm-up and rehearsal time and the start of liturgy, you should always take 5–10 minutes to spend in quiet prayer or meditation. If pieces of your life from outside your ministry well up and threaten to get "in the way," don't immediately push them aside. Look at them and name them, and then decide what to do. The decision generally boils down to this, inelegant though it may sound: "Use it or lose

Implicit in this whole process, of course, is the assumption that "on time" for a cantor means arriving early enough to rehearse anything needed and have plenty of time at the end to spend in reflection.

it." If whatever is happening in your life, at the forefront of your heart, is something you can keep there and offer up as part of what you are there to do, then don't be afraid to let it stay there. You are there to minister, but you are also there to pray and worship and be fed by the God who loves and calls us all. Sometimes the very vulnerabilities of life can deepen and enrich your ministry. Try to make them part of your prayer, bringing them forth as part of your offering upon the altar of the Eucharist. At other times, however, you may find that life's concerns keep your mind running in circles, pulling you away from prayer. When this happens, try this simple mental visualization exercise used by many artists and musicians: In your mind, put whatever it is getting in your way into a cardboard box, put a lid on it, and label it. In your mind, set it on a shelf just outside the doors of the church, and leave it there. You know it will be waiting for you when you leave; you can pick it up and deal with it then, but in the meantime it is out of your way. Go through this process until you are able to stand and be the minister you know you are called to be, and you can focus on the music and ministry await-ing you.

We have addressed how important it is to nourish your musical life outside of your function as a music minister. In the same way, an active life of prayer is important for the spirit to remain alive and healthy. The "Spirituality and Formation" section of this book (pages 16–23) will be very helpful and insightful for your personal prayer life.

The Psalms: A Cantor's Prayer Book

This book has examined in detail the cantor's role as psalmist within the liturgy. Still, it would be a mistake to let the task of proclaiming the psalms at liturgy obscure all they have to offer to cantors, as people of God and people of song. These 150 poems are filled with the hopes and joys and sorrows and longings of our brothers and sisters over millennia; they have a great deal to say to those who live and serve today. And though we know that Scripture belongs to all of God's people, you as cantors and psalmists have a unique and special relationship with these ancient songs. Read the psalms and get to know them over time. Choose one to live with daily for a week or two, depending on where your life and heart are at the time.

In a time of joy and celebration, perhaps, spend some time with Psalm 100:

> *Cry out with joy to the LORD, all the earth.*
> *Serve the LORD with gladness.*
> *Come before him, singing for joy.*[24]

When life feels uncertain or overwhelming, Psalm 121 can help quiet our souls:

> *I lift up my eyes to the mountains;*
> *from where shall come my help?*
> *My help shall come from the LORD,*
> *who made heaven and earth.*[25]

When life is at its most painful, we can seek refuge in the lament of Psalm 31:

> *Have mercy on me, O LORD;*
> *for I am in distress.*
> *My eyes are wasted with grief,*
> *my soul and my body.*[26]

Spending time with these beautiful poem-songs and becoming friends with them will not only enrich your ministry as cantors, but it will enrich your life as well.

Things to Think About

Most, when they started their ministry as cantor, weren't thinking in terms of entering into a complex and integral-to-the-liturgy ministerial role. You probably just did it because you loved to sing, or you wanted to serve your community, or someone at the parish asked you to consider leading song during liturgy, or any number of simple reasons. And once here, you discovered and continue to discover how far you've come and how much learning and growing still lies ahead.

Periodically during the liturgical year, especially if things are getting particularly busy and you begin to feel off-kilter or out of focus with your ministry, some people choose to put themselves through a very cantor-specific "examination of conscience." It will be different for everyone, but it might look something like this:

- Do I truly believe myself to be a member of the assembly?

- Do I embrace my function to support the song of the "primary choir" of the liturgy, the gathered faithful, and to help them sing with greater strength and joy?

- For cantors who sing at different liturgies in a parish: Do I sing the same way at 7:30 in the morning as at the 9:30 family-oriented Mass, or the heavily teen-populated 5:00 PM? Or do I listen to the room, trying in every second to discern what the voices before me most need from me in any given moment?

- Do I ever, when I unexpectedly hear a strong and vibrant collective voice coming from the assembly on a particular much-loved hymn, simply step away from the microphone and render myself entirely inaudible, rejoicing that in that moment I am not needed?

• When I pray before exercising my ministry, is my prayer formed as "O God, let me sing well and with beauty," or is it more like "O God, help me to become transparent and let your music and Word shine forth"?

That you would seek out further growth in your ministry is itself a sign that growth is already happening. That you understand, at whatever level of the ministry you have currently achieved, that growing and learning is a part of any ministry, is also to be affirmed and commended. The most important thing to remember, always, is that everything we do has meaning, and every smallest gesture or look or sound you make communicates something to those to whom you minister. There is no neutral ground here, no way to simply decide not to communicate something for a few minutes. You do not have the option of believing that the only time you are ministering is during the moments when we are actively singing at Mass. When you are serving as cantor for a liturgy, every moment is one of ministry.

Questions for Discussion and Reflection

1. How do you respond when people compliment you on the beauty of your voice?

_____

_____

_____

_____

_____

2. Do you experience "stage fright" before a liturgy you're preparing to serve as cantor for? If so, what are you afraid of? If the "worst" happened, whatever that means for you, what would be the consequence?

_____

_____

_____

_____

3. How would you feel if one day you realized that, with the exception of the Responsorial Psalm, your assembly was singing so well that you were in effect now obsolete and no longer needed?

_____

_____

_____

_____

4. What is your favorite part of the liturgy to sing? Why?

_____

_____

_____

_____

5. What is your favorite piece of liturgical music? Why?

_____

_____

_____

_____

6. How does your ministry as cantor and song leader/animator affect your life outside of the liturgy?

_____

_____

_____

_____

NOTES

1. See *Sing to the Lord: Music in Divine Worship* (STL), 125.

2. GIRM, 46.

3. Ibid., 47.

4. Ibid., 50.

5. Ibid., 51.

6. Ibid., 53.

7. The ordinary of the Mass is comprised of texts that do not change. They are consistent from week to week throughout the liturgy The parts of the ordinary are the Kyrie (Lord, have mercy); Gloria; Profession of Faith (Nicene or Apostles' Creed); Holy, Holy, Holy (*Sanctus*); Memorial Acclamation (with its three forms); Amen at the conclusion of the Eucharistic Prayer; and Lamb of God (*Agnus Dei*). This is in contrast to the proper of the Mass, those prayers and readings that change from week to week throughout the cycles of the liturgical year and which include the Responsorial Psalm.

8. GIRM, 51.

9. Ibid., 61.

10. See Lectionary #174.

11. GIRM, 62.

12. See ibid., 68.

13. Ibid., 78.

14. See GIRM, 88.

15. Regarding the options for singing during Communion, GIRM, 87–88 states: "In the Dioceses of the United States of America, there are four options for singing at Communion: (1) the antiphon from the Missal or the antiphon with its Psalm from the

Graduale Romanum, as set to music there or in another musical setting; (2) the antiphon with Psalm from the *Graduale Simplex* of the liturgical time; (3) a chant from another collection of Psalms and antiphons, approved by the Conference of Bishops or the Diocesan Bishop, including Psalms arranged in responsorial or metrical forms; (4) some other suitable liturgical chant (cf. no. 86) approved by the Conference of Bishops or the Diocesan Bishop. This is sung either by the choir alone or by the choir or a cantor with the people. However, if there is no singing, the antiphon given in the Missal may be recited either by the faithful, or by some of them, or by a reader; otherwise, it is recited by the Priest himself after he has received Communion and before he distributes Communion to the faithful.

"When the distribution of Communion is over, if appropriate, the Priest and faithful pray quietly for some time. If desired, a Psalm or other canticle of praise or a hymn may also be sung by the whole congregation."

16. STL, 199 states: "Although it is not necessary to sing a recessional hymn (see GIRM, 90), when it is a custom, all may join in a hymn or song after the dismissal. When a closing song is used, the procession of ministers should be arranged in such a way that it finishes during the final stanza. At times, e.g., if there has been a song after Communion, it may be appropriate to choose an option other than congregational song for the recessional. Other options include a choral or instrumental piece or, particularly during Lent, silence."

17. Some parishes blessed with sufficient cantors to do so will even separate the ministries of "Song Leader" and "Psalmist." One cantor remains at the cantor's normal location leading the singing, and the other serves strictly as a minister of the Word, proclaiming the psalm at the ambo with the lectors. While this is a wonderful idea in many ways and truly sets the psalm apart as being what it is, an integral part of the Liturgy of the Word and a sung reading from Scripture (not just a "song" that happens to fall between the readings or a "response" to the First Reading), few parishes have enough cantors to accomplish this on a regular basis.

18. A third possibility, found in the psalm collections of Joseph Gelineau, forms a sort of hybrid between the two. Gelineau's "sprung rhythm" psalmody and method for singing it are discussed in detail in Diana Kodner's *Handbook for Cantors* (published by LTP).

19. St. Augustine's *Confessions*, chapter 33.

20. "Hebrew and Greek have no separate word for music. The frontier between singing and speaking was far less precise As soon as speech turned to poetry, or when public or ceremonial speaking was involved, rhythmic and melodic features were incorporated which today would be classified as musical, or at least pre-musical." Joseph Gelineau, "Music and Singing in the Liturgy," *The Study of Liturgy*, ed. Cheslyn Jones et al., rev. ed. (New York: Oxford University Press, 1992), 497 as found in "The Cantor in Historical Perspective," *Ritual Music: Studies in Liturgical Musicology*, Edward Foley, Capuchin. (Beltsville, Maryland, Pastoral Press, 1995).

21. Obviously, "pleasant" is a highly subjective term. The fact that opera houses and rock concert stadiums tend to have radically different clienteles is testament to that! But a parish does not have a "clientele"; it is a community of faith where people gather each week to pray, give praise to God, and take part in the Eucharist. As has been mentioned before, the cantor's voice should draw attention not to itself but to the assembly it leads

and the word it proclaims. Therefore, while musicianship is paramount, it would be a mistake to assume that the most skilled and professionally trained singers will always be the best cantors. Hardworking volunteers are the backbone of the cantor ministry in the Church and not only serve their people admirably but may sometimes do a better job in the ministerial role of cantor than their professional counterparts.

22. This term means to sing not deliberately soft, with your whole voice.

23. A general guideline for microphone placement, especially for wider-ranged condenser microphones, is to never have the microphone pointed directly into the mouth—this will almost invariably cause the popping "p" problem to explode through the system. If this problem is occurring, try pointing the microphone a little higher or lower. For a shorter cantor, a microphone pointed exactly between one's eyes usually works well, and for a taller cantor sometimes the microphone pointed at the chin will solve this problem. Trial and error is the only way to find the best solution.

24. Psalm 100:1b–2.

25. Psalm 121:1–2.

26. Psalm 31:10, 11.

Frequently Asked Questions

It is important to note that any questions regarding specifics of liturgical practice for cantors are tricky to address in a general book for all cantors in every parish across the country. Your parish practice should always be the first concern, and no cantor should be unilaterally making any of these decisions on his or her own. Check with your music director, director of liturgy, and, if necessary, the pastor, who will very likely have a good sense of the prevailing dynamic of the parish staff and ministers.

However, these are important questions asked by many cantors, and they deserve to be addressed with some perspective and clarity.

1. How long should I wait to sing the psalm after the First Reading?

The Responsorial Psalm is part of the Liturgy of the Word and represents a proclamation of Scripture all on its own and is not a "response" to the First Reading. There should be enough time between the First Reading and the Responsorial Psalm (as well as between the Responsorial Psalm and the Second Reading, and the Second Reading and the Gospel Acclamation) for the assembly to breathe a bit and take in what they have just heard.[1] For some parishes, up to a full minute or more is a comfortable space for quiet contemplation; for others, more than a few moments becomes uncomfortable and unproductive.

Parishes with many families with small children will have a level of ambient noise that may inhibit true silence in a Sunday liturgy; others, with small gatherings of mostly adults, may find

> ✛ The Liturgy of the Word is to be celebrated in such a way as to favor meditation, and so any kind of haste such as hinders recollection is clearly to be avoided. In the course of it, brief periods of silence are also appropriate, accommodated to the assembled congregation; by means of these, under the action of the Holy Spirit, the Word of God may be grasped by the heart and a response through prayer may be prepared.
>
> —*General Instruction of the Roman Missal, 56*

prayerful quiet to be a very life-giving part of their communal worship. Consult with your colleagues in ministry, gauge the energy of the room, and read the silence accordingly.

2. *Do I have to walk all the way to the ambo to sing the psalm? Wouldn't it be easier to just sing it from the cantor stand?*

Easier? Of course. However, as discussed earlier in this book, the Responsorial Psalm is more than just another "song" in the liturgy; it is a piece of the proclaimed Word of God and thus holds a reverence and importance not equaled in the rest of the cantor's singing. For many years the perception has held that the psalm is merely a "response" to the First Reading; singing the psalm from the same place as the other cantor's music only reinforces this misperception. (The psalm chosen for each Sunday in the liturgical year does indeed normally reflect on and respond to the con-

> ✠ After the First Reading follows the Responsorial Psalm, which is an integral part of the Liturgy of the Word and which has great liturgical and pastoral importance, since it fosters meditation on the Word of God . . . the psalmist, or cantor of the Psalm, sings the Psalm verses at the ambo or another suitable place . . . .
>
> —*General Instruction of the Roman Missal,* 61

tent of the First Reading, but it is far more than that.) Of course, in some worship spaces concerns such as sightlines and sound delay make the ambo an impractical place to sing from; in these situations, the cantor's regular song leader location may be the best place from which to lead the psalm.

Here's a good example of how to approach the ambo. Usually, the cantor will have to move from one side of the sanctuary to the other, thus crossing in front of the altar. As noted in question #1 above, a period of silence follows the First Reading, before the psalm is sung. The cantor should be a model of this prayerful silence. When it is time, the cantor stands, and walks in a reverent pace to the altar. The cantor faces the altar, and makes a profound bow and then moves to the ambo.

The cantor should also be conscious of what kind of shoes to wear so not to create distractions when walking from one location to another. Avoid wearing shoes that might squeak when walking; that have smooth bottoms, so not to slip; or shoes with harder bottoms. Soft flats or loafers are usually a safe choice. Clothing should also be modest.

Some parishes require cantors (and choir members) to wear an alb or choir robe.

3. When should I receive Holy Communion?

The logistics of music ministry during the Communion Rite often make it difficult to discern the most appropriate time for the cantor or other music ministers to receive Holy Communion. If the cantor receives first, before the Communion Song or Chant, there can be a long lag time between the priest's reception of Holy Communion (during which, according to the GIRM, 86, the Communion Song or Chant should already have started) and the availability of a Communion minister to distribute Holy Communion to the cantor. If the cantor receives at the end of the distribution of Holy Communion, it is important that those who distribute Holy Communion wait until the Communion Song or Chant has ended and make sure the music ministers have the opportunity for the reception of Holy Communion. Specific guidelines from the pastoral staff are important here! In any case, the music ministers are still members of the gathered assembly, albeit members called forth to serve a particular function, so it is important that they be offered the same opportunity to receive the Eucharist as everyone else.[2]

> ✠ A person who has already received the Most Holy Eucharist can receive it a second time on the same day only [outside the danger of death] within the Eucharistic Celebration in which he or she participates.
>
> —*Canon Law*, §917

4. If I am cantor for more than one liturgy on a Sunday, may I receive Holy Communion at both liturgies?

Liturgical ministers who have served during one Mass and have received Holy Communion may receive Holy Communion again, if they serve during a second Mass; however, the liturgical minister is only allowed to receive twice in one day. If they happen to serve during a third Mass, they may not receive Holy Communion a third time.

5. If the assembly kneels during the Eucharistic Prayer, should I kneel or stand throughout the prayer?

The liturgical documents are generally very clear regarding proper postures for the faithful at various moments in the liturgy. If this presents a pastoral difficulty, it is probably best for the music director or director of liturgy to consult with the pastor and then communicate best practice to the cantors.

It may make pastoral sense for the cantor to remain standing during the entire Eucharistic Prayer in order to be less distracting to the assembly. Remember that in an ideal situation, wherein the assembly is familiar with and holds true ownership of the acclamations sung during the Eucharistic Prayer, you will not be needed to lead the singing at all and can simply stand or kneel with the assembly and sing from your (unamplified) place. When you are needed to bolster and support the singing, the important thing is that whatever you do be as unobtrusive as possible, so as not to draw focus away from the most important part of the rite. What this means specifically for you as a cantor will depend on many factors: The architecture of your worship space will have a lot to do with it (is the place where you stand to sing far enough from the place you would kneel that you'd need to do significant and visible walking to get there?), as will your own physical ability to kneel and stand easily and unobtrusively from your place.

> ✠ In the dioceses of the United States of America, they should kneel beginning after the singing or recitation of the *Sanctus (Holy, Holy, Holy)* until after the *Amen* of the Eucharistic Prayer, except when prevented on occasion by ill health, or for reasons of lack of space, of the large number of people present, or for another reasonable cause. However, those who do not kneel ought to make a profound bow when the Priest genuflects after the Consecration. The faithful kneel after the *Agnus Dei (Lamb of God)* unless the Diocesan Bishop determines otherwise.
>
> —*General Instruction of the Roman Missal,* 43

6. *What is the proper way to announce music during the liturgy?*

The primary concern with music announcements is that they are clear and audible. Most often a good and concise announcement of a song, chant, or hymn will go something like this: "Please join in singing number 526 from your hymnal [or name of music resource], 'Holy God, We Praise Thy Name.' Number five-two-six."

If possible, use fewer words (or preferably none at all) to announce the psalm, so that it does not lose its identity within the Liturgy of the Word and the flow of the readings is not disrupted. Many of the antiphons and refrains are brief and simple enough that assemblies can be formed over time to sing them completely from memory. Assemblies who use psalmody from weekly or periodical worship aids quickly discover that the words are there, immediately below the First Reading. If it is necessary to announce the printed location of the psalm, try to do so with as few words as possible (for example, "In the hymnal [or name of other music resource], number 35").

It is best to avoid the following announcements:

- "Welcome to our liturgy." Most or all of those gathered are presumably in their own home parish. A "welcome" such as this conveys a sense that the parish is *our* space (meaning the ministers), and we graciously welcome *them* to join us there. On major holy days or other special occasions, a friendly "We welcome all who are visiting us today, or any college students returning for the summer" better conveys a sense of welcome that is on *behalf* of the assembly, not directed toward them.

- Similarly, "Please join me in singing our Entrance Song . . . ." This phrasing, however subtly, says that *you* are doing the singing, and they are invited to sing *with* you, rather than with one another. "Let us join together in singing" or some variant is more inclusive and inviting.

- "Our Communion Song is number 55—MMMMRPH." Our voices have a natural tendency to drop in pitch—and volume—at the end of our sentences. In normal speech this is not a problem, but when announcing a three-digit number, the final digit is just as important as the first, and it must be heard clearly. Most of us must make a truly concerted effort to keep the end of the numbers as clear as the beginning. This is another reason it is helpful to state the number twice, both as a single number (557) and again as three distinct digits (five, five, seven).

- "On this glorious spring morning, with the daffodils blooming and the sun shining in the sky, let us join together in singing a joyful hymn to the God who loves us so much and has given us the gift of this beautiful day! Please turn in your hymnals to one of my personal favorite hymns, number . . . ." While it is tremendously important for you to be inviting and warm in your presentation to the assembly, you will convey most of this through presence and gesture, not through the speaking of more words. However, this example uses too many words and draws too much attention to the one doing the announcing (you, the cantor).

7. *My parish has a hymn board [or uses a worship aid]. Do I still need to announce the hymns?*

As with any procedural element you should discuss this with your music and pastoral staff. Some assemblies are accustomed enough to singing that they do not need a specific invitation to know it is time for them to sing and to participate accordingly; others require a more direct invitation. An announcement can be a helpful reminder and a nice gentle "nudge" in the direction of participation (especially at weddings and funerals); after a few years of consistent formation, the assembly may no longer need even that much. Alternatively, part of the cantor's opening greeting could include an invitation like "The numbers for all of today's music can be found on the hymn board[3] above the organ (or in the worship aid); please join in singing together."

8. *When we have a new song, should I teach it to the assembly before Mass? If so, how do I do this?*

As with everything, this will depend on your parish and its style and makeup; it will also depend on where your assembly is on the singing or not-singing continuum. When a parish is struggling with a mentality of "The cantor 'does' the music; I am not a singer, so I should just listen," frequent and even weekly rehearsals with the congregation not only serve to increase their comfort with the music, but they also reinforce the concept that the song *belongs* to the people, and that it is important to the liturgy that they sing and sing with strength and confidence. On the other hand, strong singing parishes with solid repertoires and good musical leadership will find that they can often pick up a song within a verse or so simply by following the cantor or choir, or a psalm refrain on a single hearing.

As for the "how" of teaching music to an assembly, the best way is often simply the process of "lining out" a new piece of music, where the cantor sings one phrase of the music at a time and invites the assembly to sing it back.[4] If a piece is simple enough, an entire refrain could be taught at once, but one must be careful to gauge both the assembly's learning curve and attention span: too difficult, and they can get frustrated and stop trying; too much or too long, and they can lose interest in the process. As always, read your room well. Always remember to be welcoming, and encourage the assembly with positive words and facial expressions.

Remember that before a cantor can teach the assembly a new song, the cantor first must be confident themselves with new music. If they aren't, it will be difficult for the assembly to follow, and become easily discouraged.

9. *I'm doing everything I'm supposed to do. My gestures are nice and clear, I'm secure on my music, prayerfully engaged in what I'm singing, and genuinely trying to connect with the assembly, but sometimes (or all the time!) they just don't seem to be participating. What am I doing wrong?*

While we must never cease our process of self-examination or assume that there is nothing we could do to make our ministry more effective, the truth is that of course there are *many* factors involved in whether an assembly on a particular day is able to join fully in singing the liturgy. A parish where singing is lackadaisical and unenthusiastic may take upward of five years of consistent and unflagging encouragement at *all* liturgies before it can call itself a strong and singing parish, and it is almost inevitable that even with strong leadership the process will have its moments of ebb and flow. And even in parishes that already sing with strength, some days it just does not happen as well as we would like: The weather is bad, the parish school and religious education programs have a three-day weekend, the pastor has a cold. Many things can have a negative effect on the singing on a particular day. Always remember that parish liturgy is not just an hour a week, it is an ongoing process, and that ultimately, it is about relationship—our relationships with each other as well as with the God we are there to serve.

10. What should I do differently when I cantor at weddings and funerals?

In theory, except for any music required for rite-specific moments in these special liturgies, you should not need to do anything differently at all. In practice, however, these liturgies are all too often fraught with social and familial baggage and expectations that require us not only to be even more sensitive than usual but also to function in different roles. At weddings, the social expectation is often that the person who sings is there to be a soloist, providing beautiful and relevant music to entertain and enrich a particular life event. At funerals, families are often not emotionally and spiritually in a place where they can find a voice to sing with, especially if sung liturgy has not been a major part of their past experience of Church. Both events may often serve assemblies who may not be regular churchgoers, or who come from different parishes or parts of the country or world, and who may not be formed for "full, active, and conscious participation."[5] On the other hand, funerals and weddings are key moments in people's lives that bring even those who have been away from the Church back for at least this one emotionally charged moment. The opportunity to both welcome and catechize should not be missed! Never abandon your skills of song-leading on the premise that people never sing at weddings. Don't be pushy, but continue to be inviting. Some assemblies may surprise you!

In addition to weddings and funerals, you may also be asked to cantor for other sacramental rites (such as Baptism and Confirmation), the Liturgy of the Hours, orders of blessing, devotional services (especially Eucharistic worship outside Mass), and other prayer services. While the rites may seem similar to parts of the Mass (especially the Liturgy of the Word), there are different elements and expectations. Whenever doing something new or unfamiliar make sure you meet with your music director/minister to go over the ritual in detail—this way you know exactly what to expect and you aren't thrown for a loop during the liturgy.

NOTES

1. See GIRM, 56.

2. See ibid., 86.

3. Of course, it goes without saying that if your parish is dependent on hymn boards or other large visual resources for assembly participation, these resources must be large and placed so that the entire assembly can see it!

4. Diana Kodner, in her *Handbook for Cantors,* has an excellent section on this process.

5. CSL, 14.

Resources

Please note that there is a tremendous amount of music in print today, and the needs of every parish are different. The list of suggested resources below does not include the following:
- *hymnals;*
- *annual subscription resources;*
- *bilingual and multilingual music resources.*

Each of the major publishers of music for Catholic worship carries its own selection of the above, and each has its advantages and disadvantages, many of which come down to personal taste. Serious cantors and liturgical musicians will want, over time, to build up their own library of these resources, as no single hymnal or collection has everything one could ever need.

Responsorial Psalms, Gospel Acclamations, and Prayer of the Faithful

The following publications contain all the Lectionary Responsorial Psalms and Gospel verses, along with varied Gospel Acclamation responses, needed for all Sundays and solemnities of the liturgical year. For the most part, verses are chanted to psalm tones and refrains are brief and easy to sing.

From GIA Publications

- *The Cantor's Book of Gospel Acclamations* (Guimont)

- *Cry out with Joy (Years A, B, and C)* (Haas, Harmon, Pishner, Tate, and True)

- *The Grail/Gelineau Lectionary Psalms* (Gelineau)

- *Psalms for the Revised Common Lectionary* (Guimont)

From Oregon Catholic Press (OCP)

- *Respond and Acclaim* (annual, various composers)
- *A Lectionary Psalter* (Schiavone)

From World Library Publications

- *Psalms and Ritual Music* (Years A, B, and C)
- *Lectionary Psalms and Gospel Acclamations* (Years A, B, and C)

Chant Resources

Ford, Paul. *By Flowing Waters.* Collegeville, MN: The Liturgical Press, 1999. A collection of over 700 unaccompanied chants for use in the liturgy, containing psalms, Entrance and Communion Antiphons, Mass settings (with both English and Latin versions for many of the chants), and much more. An invaluable and accessible resource for choirs, directors, and assemblies seeking to familiarize themselves with the Church's tradition of chant singing.

Psallité (Years A, B, and C). Collegeville, MN: The Liturgical Press, 2005, 2006, 2007. A comprehensive collection of psalms and antiphons for the liturgical calendar, in English, including the proper Entrance and Communion Antiphons for all Sundays of all three liturgical cycles. An excellent resource that is providing many parishes with the opportunity to reintroduce chant singing into their parish repertoire.

The Roman Gradual/*Graduale Romanum* (Solesmes). Available through many different publishers, this is the primary collection of Latin chant, including the propers for the entire liturgical year, the ritual and votive Masses, the sanctoral cycle, the complete "Kyriale," and the collection of all the chants for seventeen different Mass settings as well as additional music. The volume is entirely in Latin, and the chants are in "neume" (four-line) notation.

Tortolano, William. *A Gregorian Chant Handbook*. Chicago, IL: GIA Publications, 2005. A clear and concise guide to learning to read chant (square-note, or neumatic) notation for the person with no prior experience.

Music Development Resources

Breedlove, Jennifer Kerr. *Sight-Sing a New Song*. Franklin Park, IL: World Library Publications, 2004. Designed both for classroom use and for self-study with a keyboard, this method gives a basic introduction to the skills of sight-reading and musical notation, specifically geared to the needs of the volunteer singer. Also now available in Spanish: *Aprende a leer la musica*, translated by Marieth Quintero, 2011.

Conable, Barbara H. and Benjamin J. Conable. *What Every Musician Needs to Know about the Body*. Chicago, IL: GIA Publications, Inc., 1998, 2000. Based on a six-hour course of the same name, this book explains an approach to healthy and efficient use of the human skeletal and musculature systems, known as "body mapping." This book relies on illustrations, diagrams, and charts to give a very clear and understandable explanation of the workings of the entire body.

Ferris, William. *The Care and Feeding of Singers: A Handbook of Choral Vocalises*. Frankling Park, IL: World Library Publications, 1993. A collection of vocal exercises aimed at developing healthy vocal techniques for singers as well as honing listening and intonation skills within a larger group.

Van de Graaff, Kathleen. *Winning Warm-ups for the Voice*. Skokie IL: Domenico Productions, Inc., 1999. A sixty-minute CD of vocal warm-ups for singers enabling the singer to vocalize systematically through all parts of their registers without use of a piano. Available in versions for female high voice, female low voice, male high voice, and male low voice. A second CD, *More Winning Warm-ups for the Voice*, is also available, as is a ninety-two-page book titled *A Systematic Approach to Voice Exercises* (also by Kathleen Van de Graaff).

Liturgical Resources

General Instruction of the Roman Missal. USCCB Publishing, 2010. The basic "handbook" for how to do liturgy in the Roman Catholic Church, with a great deal of information regarding sacred music. Basic reading for any Roman Catholic, especially one involved in ministry of any kind. Available in LTP's *The Liturgy Documents, Fifth Edition, Volume 1.*

Sourcebook for Sundays, Seasons, and Weekdays. Chicago, IL: Liturgy Training Publications, annual. An annual resource that provides information about the seasons and daily liturgical observances. Helpful for familiarization with Roman Catholic liturgy.

Truitt, Gordon E., editor. *The Way We Worship: Pastoral Reflections on the General Instruction of the Roman Missal.* Washington, DC: National Pastoral Musicians, 2003. A collection of articles from "A General Instruction Primer" to items on liturgical catechesis, music, liturgical law, and pastoral theology designed to give ministers a clear, readable, easily grasped view of the *General Instruction of the Roman Missal.*

Prayer Resources

At Home with the Word®. Chicago, IL: Liturgy Training Publications, annual. An annual resource providing insights regarding the Scriptures for Sundays.

Haas, David. *With Every Note I Sing.* Chicago, IL: GIA Publications, 1995. A prayer book for cantors and vocalists.

Hommerding, Alan J. *Blessed Are the Music Makers.* Franklin Park, IL: World Library Publications, 2004. Unlike most other collections of prayers for music ministers, this book is specifically intended to provide immediately accessible, seasonally relevant, brief, and musically rewarding prayer services suitable for beginning or ending rehearsals or meetings. An invaluable resource!

Fragomeni, Richard. *In Shining Splendor.* Franklin Park, IL: World Library Publications, 2006. Reflections and meditations on the *Exsultet.*

Hommerding, Alan. *In Holy Harmony: Prayeres for Parish Musicians* Franklin Park, IL: World Library Publicaitons, 2009. This collection includes many of the same prayers found in *Blessed Are the Music Makers,* in a simple text-only format and removed from the prayer service format of the original resource.

Nowak, Michael. *Called to Be Your Song: Prayers for Cantors.* Franklin Park, IL: World Library Publications, 2010. A collection of both seasonal and occasion-specific prayers written for those who serve in cantor ministry.

Prayers for Those Who Make Music. Chicago, IL: Liturgy Training Publications, 1996. A prayer book for cantors, choir members, instrumentalists, and choir directors.

Truitt, Gordon E. *A Pastoral Musician's Book of Days.* Washington, DC: National Pastoral Musicians, 2000. Generally following the Roman calendar for feasts and memorials, this book includes reflections not only for those saints we would normally expect but also marks the birthdates of composers such as Praetorius and Verdi, as well as key people such as Charles Wesley and Martin Luther King Jr.

For Further Reading

Connolly, Michael. *The Parish Cantor: Helping Catholics Pray in Song.* Chicago, IL: GIA Publications, 1991. Another farily comprehensive volume covering the major aspects of the cantor's ministry. Though more than twenty years old, it still contains much valuable information.

Eustis, Lynn. *The Singer's Ego: Finding Balance Between Music and Life,* Chicago, IL: GIA Publications, Inc., 2005. An acclaimed singer and voice teacher, in this very personal memoir-like account of her own experiences, addresses many of the concerns unique to vocal musicians.

Haas, David. *Music and the Mass, Second Edition.* Chicago, IL: Liturgy Training Publications, 2013. A basic guide to key documents and principles regarding the celebration of the Eucharist. It walks through the

Mass, rite by rite and step by step, describing each part through Scripture, Church documents, and various other sources. The author also offers commentary about the meaning of each part of the Mass through the lens of liturgical music.

Hanson, Jim, Melanie Coddington, and Joe Simmons. *Cantor Basics, Revised Edition.* Portland, OR: Oregon Catholic Press, 2003. This revised classic provides liturgical information, recruitment strategies, technical skills, and spiritual tips for cantors.

Jordan, James: *The Musician's Soul Trilogy:* Chicago, IL: GIA Publications, 1999, 2002, 2006.
- *The Musician's Soul: A Journey Examining Spirituality for Performers, Teachers, Composers, Conductors, and Music Educators* (1999)
- *The Musician's Spirit: Connecting to Others through Story* (2002)
- *The Musician's Walk: An Ethical Labyrinth* (2006)

Each book in this trilogy by renowned conductor James Jordan is like a retreat on paper, deserving of being read and reread, with quotes from musicians and others interspersed with Dr. Jordan's own reflections on music and music-making.

Kodner, Diana. *Handbook for Cantors.* Chicago, IL: Liturgy Training Publications, 1997. A must for anyone in the cantor ministry; this book includes more information regarding psalm tones, gesturing, weddings and funerals, how to teach music to an assembly, and much more.

Truitt, Gordon, editor. *Psalmist and Cantor: A Pastoral Music Resource.* Washington, DC: National Pastoral Musicians, 2005. A slim volume containing seven brief articles about aspects of the ministry of the cantor such as being psalmist, preserving vocal health, animating assembly song, recruitment of young cantors, and so on.

Video Resources

I Will Call God's Name. Chicago, IL: GIA Publications, Inc., 1995. This two-volume VHS tape set features David Hass and Bonnie Faber presenting a workshop on cantor skills.

Teach Us to Pray: Praying the Psalms. Cincinnati, OH: St. Anthony Messenger Press, 2000. This video from the *Catholic Update* series presents catechesis, stories, and witness about the psalms in Roman Catholic liturgy. This video features composer David Haas.

Organizations

National Association of Pastoral Musicians (NPM)
962 Wayne Avenue, Suite 210
Silver Spring, MD 20910-4461
www.npm.org

American Guild of Organists
475 Riverside Drive, Suite 1260
New York, NY 10115
www.agohq.org

Music Publishers

GIA Publications, Inc.
7404 South Mason Avenue
Chicago, IL 60638
www.giamusic.com

The Liturgical Press
Saint John's Abbey
PO Box 7500
Collegeville, MN 56321-7500
www.litpress.org

Oregon Catholic Press (OCP)
5536 NE Hassalo
Portland, OR 97213-3638
www.ocp.org

World Library Publications (WLP)
J. S. Paluch Company, Inc.
3708 River Rd. Suite 400
Franklin Park, IL 60131
www.wlpmusic.com

Glossary

ACCLAMATION BEFORE THE GOSPEL: Normally accompanies the procession with the *Book of the Gospels*. In this song of praise, the assembly "welcomes and greets the Lord who is about to speak to them in the Gospel."[1] It consists of an assembly response ("Alleluia" for most of the year, which is replaced by a different response during Lent[2]) and a Gospel verse, usually intoned by the cantor. It is often referred to as the Gospel Acclamation.

ANTIPHON: A brief refrain, with or without chanted psalm verses, sung at the Entrance, Offertory, or Communion of the Eucharistic Liturgy. Antiphons also precede and follow each of the psalms and canticles in the Liturgy of the Hours. (Please also see entry for "Response/Antiphon/Refrain").

ANTIPHONAL FORM: From the Greek *antiphonon*, ("sounding against" or "singing opposite"), this style of singing usually involves a back-and-forth singing of one group in alternation with another.

ASSEMBLY: All those who gather for liturgical worship make up the assembly, the Body of Christ, the Church. However, the assembly is ordered hierarchically, arranged by rank and function.

CANTICLE: Any scriptural song *not* found in the Book of Psalms. These form an integral part of the Liturgy of the Hours and are often found in our Sunday worship as well, taking the place of the Responsorial Psalm. Examples of scriptural canticles found in the Sunday Lectionary are the *Magnificat* (Luke 1:46–55) and the Canticle of Daniel or the Canticle of the Three Children (Daniel 3:57–88).

CANTOR: The minister of the sung or chanted prayers for a worshipping community. In the Roman Catholic Church, the cantor has three distinct functions: as song leader or animator, he or she leads and assists the assembly in their music; as psalmist, he or she proclaims the sung Responsorial Psalm as part of the Liturgy of the Word; and when there is no leadership necessary, he or she functions simply as a member of the assembly, modeling the participation to which all are invited.

CHANT (OR PLAINCHANT): Often incorrectly used as synonymous with the term "Gregorian chant," this more general term refers to any form of vocal music which is sung without specific rhythmic values assigned to individual notes; its rhythmic impetus is usually driven by the text.[3] The term "chant," as a translation of the Latin *cantus*, is also used throughout the *General Instruction on the Roman Missal* to refer to most pieces of music throughout the liturgy.

CHANT NOTATION: The precursor to our contemporary musical notation. Chant notation, also called "neume" or "neumatic" notation, had four staff lines instead of five; the shape of the note-heads (called "neumes") indicated the relative length of the note.

COMMUNION ANTIPHON: Please see entry for "Antiphon."

CONSTITUTION ON THE SACRED LITURGY *(SACROSANCTUM CONCILIUM)*: "In the reform and promotion of the liturgy, this full and active participation by all the people is the aim to be considered before all else. For it is the primary and indispensable source from which the faithful are to derive the true Christian spirit . . . ."[4] The first document of the Second Vatican Council, which forms the basis for all our corporate worship and includes sections on the participation of the assembly, liturgical inculturation, the Liturgy of the Hours, the liturgical year, and sacred music and art.

DIVINE OFFICE: Please see entry for "Liturgy of the Hours."

ENTRANCE ANTIPHON: Please see entry for "Antiphon."

EUCHARISTIC ACCLAMATIONS: The moments during the Eucharistic Prayer that invite the assembly's response. These consist of the *Sanctus* (Holy, Holy, Holy), the Memorial Acclamation, and the Amen and the acclamations in Masses with children. The *Sanctus* and Amen always use the same text. The options for the Memorial Acclamation include "We proclaim your Death, O Lord, / and profess your Resurrection / until you come again"; "When we eat this Bread and drink this Cup, / we proclaim your Death, O Lord, / until you come again"; and "Save us, Saviour of the world, / for by your Cross and Resurrection / you have set us free."

EUCHARISTIC PRAYER: The prayer that is "the center and high point of the entire celebration begins"[5] immediately following the preparation of the altar with the Preface dialogue: "The Lord be with you . . ." and continues unbroken through the Amen as a single prayer. Its elements usually include thanksgiving, acclamation, *anamnesis* (making present the memory of Christ's meal and sacrifice), institution narrative (the retelling of the Last Supper), petition, and the final doxology ("Through him, and with him, and in him . . . ,") culminating in the Amen.

GENERAL INSTRUCTION OF THE ROMAN MISSAL (GIRM): The document of the Roman Catholic Church dealing specifically with the celebration of the Mass. It contains highly specific instructions regarding almost every area of the Eucharistic liturgy, including those parts of the liturgy that incorporate music. The primary reference document for discovering almost any aspect of liturgical celebration. It is the introductory document found in *The Roman Missal.*

GLORIA: Hymn of praise sung as part of the Introductory Rites of the Mass at all Sunday celebrations outside of Lent and Advent, and at all solemnities and feasts.[6]

GREGORIAN CHANT: A specific body of music from the Middle Ages, written in chant (or "plainchant") form. Generally ascribed by legend to St. Gregory the Great, this body of chant makes up the bulk of the extant music we have from the earlier centuries of the Roman Church. Gregorian chant is "distinctive of the Roman liturgy . . . it should be given pride of place in liturgical services."[7]

HYMN (STROPHIC HYMN): Musical form in which the melody for a verse is repeated several times with different text for each verse, or "strophe" (for example, "Joy to the World").

LEADER OF SONG: A function of the cantor. The leader of song is primarily responsible for fostering musical participation from the assembly through strong musical leadership, proper gesture, facial expression, and invitation.

LITANIC FORM: In the form of a litany. (Please also see "Responsorial Form.")

LITANY: A call-and-response petitionary prayer—such as the Universal Prayer (Prayer of the Faithful); Litany of the Saints; or the Kyrie (Lord, Have Mercy)—in which petitions sung or recited by a cantor or leader alternate with a brief fixed response by the assembly.

LITURGY: From the Greek *leitourgia,* originally meaning a public act (the "work of the people") performed for the good of the community. In the Roman Catholic Church, the word is used in reference to any of the official rites of the Church as found in the Roman ritual books. This would include, for example, the Liturgy of the Hours, Word services, and celebrations of sacraments (Baptism, Marriage) within and outside of Mass, as well as the Liturgy of the Eucharist.[8]

LITURGY OF THE EUCHARIST: Begins with the Preparation of the Gifts and includes the Eucharistic Prayer with its acclamations, Rite of Communion, and Prayer after Communion.

LITURGY OF THE HOURS: Also known as the "Divine Office," this is the cycle of prayers, psalms, and canticles specified for the specific hours of the day. Originally consisting of eight different daily prayer times (Matins, Lauds, Prime, Terce, Sext, None, Vespers, and Compline). Morning Prayer (Lauds) and Evening Prayer (Vespers) are the "chief hours," the "two hinges on which the daily office turns."[9] Each office contains hymns, psalms, canticles, petitions, and other prayers.

LITURGY OF THE WORD: The first of the two main parts of the Mass, which encompasses the readings from Scripture, the singing of the psalm, the proclamation of the Gospel, the Homily, the Profession of Faith, and the Universal Prayer.

NEUME: Note-head used in Chant Notation (please see "Chant Notation").

OFFERTORY SONG: The song sung as the gifts are brought forward and the altar prepared for the celebration of the Eucharist.

ORDINARY: The liturgical texts that remain unchanged from Sunday to Sunday. These include the *Kyrie eleison* (Lord, have mercy), the Gloria, the Profession of Faith or Creed (or *Credo*), the *Sanctus* (Holy, Holy, Holy), and the *Agnus Dei* (Lamb of God).

PRELUDE: A piece of music played or sung prior to the entrance song of a liturgy. It is not a formal part of any liturgical rites.

PROPER: Texts in the liturgy that change week to week based on the liturgical calendar. These include the readings from Scripture; the Responsorial Psalm; the Entrance and Communion Antiphons; and many of the presidential prayers.

PSALM: Any of the 150 poem-songs from the Book of Psalms in the Old Testament.

PSALM TONE: A simple melodic formula used for chanting the verses of psalms.

PSALMIST: The role taken by the cantor during the proclamation of the Responsorial Psalm. This moment is distinct from other parts of the cantor's ministry. Here, the cantor is a minister of the Word, proclaiming Scripture in song.

REFRAIN: Please see entry for "Response/Antiphon/Refrain."

RESPONSE/ANTIPHON/REFRAIN: These three terms tend to be used almost interchangeably in the contemporary Church, although each has a slightly different connotation. "Refrain" is a musical term (referring to structure), "Response" is a functional term, and "Antiphon" is a liturgical term. Normally, "Antiphon" is reserved for specific moments in the liturgy (please see entry for "antiphon") and for the psalms in the Divine Office. In the Responsorial Psalm, the terms "refrain" and "response" are often used synonymously by different publishers and musicians, although the term "response" may be preferable in that it connotes the dialogic nature of the psalm in a way that "refrain" does not. For the same reason, the people's part in a litany is usually referred to as a "response." When speaking about a song in verse-refrain form, obviously, the term "refrain" would be used.

RESPONSORIAL FORM: A dialogic form of singing alternating between cantor and assembly. Most easily identified in the singing of the Responsorial Psalm, in which the cantor proclaims the psalm verses and the people respond with their fixed refrain, this form can also be used at other points in the liturgy. (Litanic form is a subcategory of responsorial form, in which the cantor's part forms a petitionary prayer and the people's response is usually quite brief.)

RITUAL MUSIC/SACRED MUSIC: Any music that forms an integral part of the Roman Catholic liturgy. "The musical tradition of the universal Church is a treasure of inestimable value, greater even than that of any other art . . . . Therefore sacred music will be the more holy the more closely it is joined to the liturgical rite."[10]

ROMAN GRADUAL: Contains the chants for the ordinary and proper of the Mass.

ROMAN MISSAL: The complete texts and rubrics used for the celebration of the Mass in the Roman rite.

SACRED MUSIC: Please see "Ritual Music."

SACROSANCTUM CONCILIUM: Please see *Constitution on the Sacred Liturgy.*

SEASONAL RESPONSORIAL PSALM: The Lectionary makes provision for certain psalms to replace the weekly "proper" psalms for those parishes for whom learning the entire cycle of psalmody would be too difficult. Several psalms are specified for use during different seasons of the liturgical year.

SEQUENCE: A liturgical hymn sung immediately following the second reading. A sequence is sung on the Solemnities of Easter Sunday (and throughout the Octave), Pentecost, Most Holy Body and Blood of Christ (*Corpus Christi*), and the memorial of Our Lady of Sorrows. Please note that it is only required on Easter Sunday and Pentecost.[11]

SIMPLE GRADUAL: Contains alternate antiphons for the Entrance, Offertory, and Communion Chants. They are simpler melodies than those in the Roman Gradual.

SING TO THE LORD: MUSIC IN DIVINE WORSHIP (**STL**): The 2007 document from the United States Bishops' Committee on the Liturgy addressing issues of music ministry following the Second Vatican Council.

SONG FORM: Also known as "verse-refrain" form. Musical form in which verses (with identical melody but different texts) of music alternate with a consistent refrain (identical melody and text). Examples include "Blest Are They" and "On Eagle's Wings."

STROPHE: One verse, or stanza, of a strophic hymn. (Please see "hymn.")

THROUGH-COMPOSED FORM: Term commonly given to pieces of music with no set repetitions or refrains. In the liturgy, this form is the Eucharistic acclamation, and sometimes the Gloria.

UNIVERSAL PRAYER: Litanic prayer of petition offered by the gathered assembly, offered for the Church, the world, the oppressed, and the local community. The final element that closes the Liturgy of the Word at the Mass. It is also called the Prayer of the Faithful and Bidding Prayers.

NOTES

1. GIRM, 62.

2. Many Lenten acclamations are provided in the Lectionary, 223, 1–8.

3. Please note that the term "chant" will find other usage, especially in world music and the songs of Taizé, where this definition might not apply.

4. CSL, 14.

5. GIRM, 78.

6. The Gloria should not be sung during Advent and Lent with the exception of the Solemnities of the Immaculate Conception of the Blessed Virgin Mary, Saint Joseph, and the Annunciation as well as the feasts of Our Lady of Guadalupe and the Chair of Saint Peter.

7. CSL, 116.

8. It should be noted that in the Eastern churches, the term "liturgy" or "Divine Liturgy" refers *only* to the celebration of the Eucharist. The word "Mass" is not a part of their tradition.

9. CSL, 89A.

10. CSL, 112.

11. See GIRM, 64.

Let All Things Now Living

1. Let all things now living
    A song of thanksgiving
    To God our Creator triumphantly raise;
    Who fashioned and made us,
    Protected and stayed us,
    By guiding us onto the end of our days.
    God's banners are o'er us,
    Pure light goes before us,
    A pillar of fire shining forth in the night:
    Till shadows have vanished
    And darkness is banished,
    As forward we travel from light into Light.

2. His law he enforces,
    The stars in their courses,
    The sun in its orbit obediently shine,
    The hills and the mountains,
    The rivers and fountains,
    The depths of the ocean proclaim God divine.
    We, too, should be voicing
    Our love and rejoicing
    With glad adoration,
    a song let us raise:
    Till all things now living
    Unite in thanksgiving,
    To God in the highest, hosanna and praise.

Psalm 71:3–4a, 5–6ab, 16–17

R. (See 8) *My mouth shall be filled with your praise,*
and I will sing your glory!

Be my rock of refuge,
  a stronghold to give me safety,
  for you are my rock and my fortress.
O my God, rescue me from the hand of
    the wicked.

R. *My mouth shall be filled with your praise,*
and I will sing your glory!

For you are my hope, O Lord;
  my trust, O God, from my youth.
On you I depend from birth;
  from my mother's womb you are my strength.

R. *My mouth shall be filled with your praise,*
and I will sing your glory!

I will treat of the mighty works of the Lord;
  O God, I will tell of your singular justice.
O God, you have taught me from my youth,
  and till the present I proclaim your wondrous deeds.

R. *My mouth shall be filled with your praise,*
and I will sing your glory!